in·fi·del·i·ty

The Best Worst Thing that Could Happen to Your Marriage

By

Talal H. Alsaleem, LMFT

Infidelity Recovery Specialist

Illuminare Creations

Published

2017

Printed in the United States of America

First Printing, 2017

ISBN 0-6928748-2-8

Illuminare Creations
9984 Niblick Drive, Suite #2
Roseville, CA 95747

www.IllulminareCreations.com

This book contains information that is intended to help the
readers be better informed consumers of mental health services.
It is presented as general advice on mental health services.
Always consult your therapist or psychiatrist for your individual
needs.

This book is not intended to be a substitute for the mental health
advice of a licensed therapist or psychiatrist. The reader should
consult with their mental health professional in any matter
relating to his/her mental health.

The author has made every effort to ensure the accuracy of the
information within this book was correct at the time of
publication. The author does not assume and hereby disclaims
any liability to any party for any loss, damage, or disruption
caused by errors or omissions, whether such errors or omissions
result from accident, negligence, or any other cause.

Dedication

For my wife Angela and her relentless love and support,

For my daughter Sabiha and her inspiring tenacity,

For all my clients and their bravery of spirit,

Thank you all for making this possible.

Table of Contents

Part I: Understanding Infidelity

Chapter 1: Introduction: 3

❖ Why Is Infidelity the Best Worst Thing that Could Happen to a
   Marriage? 4
❖ A Message to the Betrayed 10
❖ A Message to the Unfaithful 13
❖ Why Is It Important to Process Infidelity? 16

Chapter 2: Definition and Stats 20

❖ What Is Infidelity? 21
❖ Types of Affairs 22
❖ Infidelity and Mental Illness 24
❖ Infidelity and Sex Addiction 28
❖ Infidelity and Sexual Identity 29
❖ Infidelity Statistics and Facts 30

Chapter 3: Causes of Infidelity 37

❖ Why Does Infidelity Happen? 38
❖ Different Types of Causes 41

Part II: Healing from Infidelity

Chapter 4: The First Milestone, Setting the Stage for Healing 52

❖ Step 1: Making a Conscious Choice 53
❖ Step 2: Agreeing on the Logistics 57
❖ Step 3: Anticipating and Preparing for Challenges 59
❖ Step 4: Seeking Professional Help 65

Chapter 5: The Second Milestone, Getting the Story 69

❖ Why Is It Important to Get the Story? 70
❖ The Trifecta of Truth 71
❖ Things to Keep in Mind 79

Chapter 6: The Third Milestone, Acknowledging the Impact 81

- ❖ The Benefits of Acknowledging the Impact of
  Infidelity 83
- ❖ Impact of Infidelity 85
- ❖ Concrete Steps to Acknowledge the Impact of
  Infidelity 91
- ❖ Challenges and Pitfalls 95

Chapter 7: The Forth Milestone, Choosing a Path 101

- ❖ Why Do Couples Get Stuck? 103
- ❖ The Choices You Have in Front of You 112
- ❖ How to Choose a Path? 113

Chapter 8: The Fifth Milestone, Creating a Plan of Action 118

- ❖ Prerequisites for the Plans of Action 120
- ❖ Qualities of a Successful Plan of Action 123
- ❖ The Action Plan for Separation 127
- ❖ The Action Plan for Rebuilding 134
- ❖ Goal Setting Example 142

**Chapter 9: The Sixth Milestone, Implementation and Healing
Pains** 145

- ❖ Rules of Successful Implementation 146
- ❖ Healing Pains 150

**Chapter 10: The Seventh Milestone, Monitoring and
Sustainability** 166

- ❖ What Is Sustainability? 167
- ❖ Achieving Sustainability 170
- ❖ Prevention 173
- ❖ Intervention 177
- ❖ Final Words 180

Milestone Progress Chart 184

PART I

Understanding Infidelity

Chapter 1

Introduction

"Losing the possibility of something is the exact same thing as losing hope and without hope nothing can survive."

---Mark Z Danielewski

The controversial title of this book was not chosen for shock value, but to simply illustrate the undisputed fact that infidelity is the rudest and most unpleasant wakeup call one can receive to get the message that something is seriously wrong in their relationship.

Why Is It the Worst Thing that Could Happen to a Marriage?

Well, because it's one of the most painful and selfish acts that one partner can commit against another. We are all susceptible to acting selfishly at times, which can cause direct or indirect pain to the people we love. But, infidelity is not your run-of-the-mill, selfish type of behavior most of us engage in throughout our relationships. It might be motivated by similar forces such as the real or imagined feeling of unfulfilled needs, but the impact that it causes is far more devastating than ordinary acts of selfishness, because it damages the most important pillar that is needed to sustain a strong foundation to a healthy and happy relationship: the sense of security in ourselves and our relationships. When infidelity happens, it shakes this foundation of security by challenging our feelings of trust and adequacy.

Feelings of Trust

Infidelity, by definition, cannot occur without the element of deceit. Deceit is the conscious act of dishonesty and comes in many shapes and flavors ranging from the seemingly harmless omission of truth ("I didn't know that you wanted to know that sometimes I flirt with my co-workers") to the flat out lie (you say, "I am going on a business trip," when in fact you are spending the night somewhere else). Deceit and trust are like the opposite ends of a magnet; they can never be aligned in the same field, no matter how hard you try to make those ends meet.

Marriages in particular and relationships in general are different types of partnerships that are formed for the purpose of fulfilling emotional and physical needs that we all have in order to live a happy existence. In order for any partnership to succeed, there has to be a level of trust between partners to allow the two to work together to achieve the main goals of the partnership. The act of infidelity requires deceit, deceit equals dishonesty, and dishonesty leads to mistrust. Without trust you cannot have a successful partnership.

Feelings of Adequacy

We are all born with the natural need and desire to feel adequate or *good enough*. Some of us even strive for going above and beyond *good enough* to achieve the status of *great, amazing,* or *extraordinary*.

What makes the act of infidelity stand out from other selfish behaviors is the fact that it requires the involvement of a third party, someone other than our partner to accomplish the goals of the selfish behaviors. This automatically sets the stage for a comparison between the partner who was betrayed and the person, or persons, who the unfaithful involved in the affair. This comparison almost always leads the partner who was betrayed to question their adequacy and self-worth, which is by far one of the worst feelings one can experience in a relationship. Think of it this way, nobody likes to hear that they are not good enough, regardless of the truth of such a statement. It's even worse to hear someone say, "You are not good enough and that's why I went behind your back to get my needs met by someone else, who I believe is better than you in that department."

Interestingly enough, in the majority of cases of infidelity the unfaithful is not cheating because their partner is not good enough. Infidelity is caused by a more complicated set of circumstances related to the unfaithful's ability to identify unfulfilled needs and the ability to communicate to their partner about those needs, a topic we will discuss in detail in the next chapters.

Why Is It the Best Worst Thing that Could Happen to a Marriage?

The notion that infidelity can be the best thing that ever happened to your relationship can be described as absurd, to say the least. Most people struggle with this idea because of the tremendous amount of pain and destruction caused by the affair, which rightfully overshadows any possibility for seeing any silver lining. It's almost as absurd as telling someone to rejoice and celebrate that they found out that the house they built, love, and live in is infested with termites, and somehow this termite problem is the best thing that ever happened to their house. If you know anything about home ownership stressors, this has to be in the top three types of bad news you can receive about your house.

For the record, I am not recommending infidelity and affairs as a homeopathic remedy to fix your marriage and your relationship problems. I am simply highlighting the fact that a painful, destructive act can give couples a rare opportunity to rebuild their relationship to be better, stronger, and more fulfilling than it was prior to the affair.

How is this accomplished? Ironically, the trauma and pain caused by infidelity is what provides the couples with two main elements needed to for a second chance: system shock and a nothing-to-lose attitude. These two elements create the best environment for a second chance.

System Shock

Most of us are aware of the lifestyle choices and unhealthy patterns of behavior that make us unhappy. These choices and behaviors cause us minor aches and pains which most of us tend to ignore in the hope that the problems will find a way of working themselves out, or that we would learn to live with the pain instead of seeking medical attention. The only time we seek assistance is if we are experiencing some major symptoms, or we are forced into going to the emergency room because of the severity of the pain and discomfort we are experiencing.

This pattern of behavior carries over to how couples deal with relationship problems. A lot of the time, couples know that something is off, but they are not sure that it's significant enough to warrant seeking help, or they think that it's just a normal reaction to current life stressors. They might also mistakenly think it's a normal relationship rut that couples get stuck in after many years of being together. After many more small problems, down the road those issues accumulate and cause further damage to the relationship.

For example, most of us will ignore an irregular blood pressure reading and attribute it to stress or other factors and hope it will work itself out instead of going to see our primary care physician. But we will drop everything and seek urgent help, if we are experiencing any signs and symptoms that can be attributed to a heart attack.

Infidelity is like a heart attack, because it's caused by the accumulation of many minor, untreated problems, poor decisions, and unhealthy lifestyle choices. Plus, its impact is very serious and life threatening to a point that forces couples to seriously evaluate their relationship and have a final chance to take extreme measures to save it.

The seriousness of this system shock is what snaps the couple out of the auto pilot attitude they had to life which caused them to ignore the minor problems they were experiencing in their relationship prior to the act of infidelity.

Now, for the first time in God knows when, they are awake and very aware of the fact that there is something seriously wrong in the relationship that requires immediate attention. This will force the couple to evaluate how they got here.

Nothing-to-Lose Attitude

When people find out that they are diagnosed with a serious, life-threatening condition such as heart disease, they undergo a series of emotional reactions that leads to the development of a nothing-to-lose attitude. The same is true when people are dealing with infidelity. The nothing-to-lose attitude can become a double-edged sword, however; some people use it as an excuse to give up and run away from their problems and the hard choices they have to make to correct it. Others will embrace it, and use it as a platform for a fierce survival campaign aimed at doing whatever it takes to survive the act of infidelity and rebuild the relationship to be stronger and better than it ever was.

If you don't believe me, look at all the stories of overcoming adversity and challenges that people undergo once their survival is threatened. Some make miraculous, life-changing decisions, and others give up and surrender to adversity.

The nothing-to-lose attitude gives the couple a rare opportunity to be completely open and honest with each other about what went wrong simply because the worst thing that could ever happen to their relationship has already happened. This means there is no more need for hiding, ignoring, and lying about the circumstances that led to infidelity. Because, either way, the motivation for dishonesty is removed. In this situation, dishonesty will become an obstacle that will prevent you from getting unstuck in either path you choose, whether you decide to build the relationship or end it.

If a couple chooses to rebuild, then they are able to rebuild on a fresh, clean slate with total awareness and understanding of all the pitfalls that caused the relationship to deteriorate. If the couple chooses to end the relationship, then they owe it to themselves and to each other to walk away with a clear understanding of why the relationship failed so that they can learn from the mistakes they made in this relationship to avoid repeating them in the future.

***

A Message to the Betrayed:

It takes a lot of guts and courage to even consider the prospect of fixing your relationship, especially when you feel that your heart has been torn out of your chest and has been repeatedly stomped on as the result of the act of infidelity, the same ugly act that caused you to feel unimaginable amounts of pain, anger, resentment, disgust, confusion, and fear.

Yet you are still here, reading this book, despite the protests of every molecule in your body screaming, "Leave this cheating @!#%*&!" The fact that you are here taking steps to understand what happened and why it happened is a reflection of your courage and resiliency.

Believe it or not, the easiest thing to do is to run away and never look back, which is what most people do. It's easier because it's the path of least resistance when dealing with the intense feelings of anger, pain, and fear you are experiencing as a result of the affair. It's easier, because it allows you to do what seems to be a rational choice that will protect you from ever being hurt again by your partner, as well as protect your pride and ego, which are doing a great job preventing you from even considering the possibility of attempting to salvage this relationship by saying things like, "Only a doormat would stay put," or, "Don't you have any respect for yourself?"

Here is the deal: I could sit here and give you my spiel about taking the road less travelled, and the value of making the right choices which are not always easy to make, but I don't think that would be an argument with enough weight to compete against the intensity of the feelings you are experiencing, urging you to go in the opposite direction. But what I can do instead is remove the main obstacle that prevents people in your shoes to even consider another option besides running away. That obstacle is fear.

When we are betrayed by our partners we face three main fears: fear of staying in the relationship for the wrong reason, fear of not being able to fully recover from the affair, and the fear of getting hurt again. All of these fears are a very normal reaction to the trauma of infidelity, and the only way to address those fears is by offering the following assurances:

One: Reading this book does not mean that you already made a commitment to saving the relationship. The only commitment I need from you at this point is a commitment to the process of understanding what happened, why it happened, and where to go from here. This will guarantee that whatever choice you and your partner make will be motivated by the right reasons.

Two: Many of the couples I have worked with were able to successfully heal from the devastating impact of infidelity and were able to rebuild their relationship to be even stronger than they ever imagined. It's not an easy process and requires a lot of effort from both parties, but it's achievable if the couple is able to be honest with themselves and each other about their expectations and their willingness to meet those expectations. Right now, it's really hard to imagine how it's even possible to get past such an unforgettable event. Healing does not mean forgetting, because you can never erase a painful memory. The next best thing is for the memory to fade away as time passes and trust is rebuilt. Think of it as an ugly site that you leave behind as you move forward, kind of like an image in a rearview mirror that gets smaller and smaller as you drive away. Eventually, that painful memory will become nothing more than an insignificant speck.

Three: As for the fear of getting hurt again, no one can guarantee this won't happen because of the simple fact that we are human, we are flawed, and we make mistakes. This is an unavoidable truth, whether or not you decide to stay in this relationship or move on to another one. The only guarantee that I can give you is this: if you and your partner learn to identify your needs, learn to communicate about those needs effectively, and make the necessary compromises to meet those needs throughout the life cycle of your relationship, then you will never have to find yourself in this position again because there simply wouldn't be a reason for it.

I hope that reading this message is giving you the reassurance that you need to begin the journey of healing, not only for your partner's and family's sake, but for yours, because you matter and deserve to heal and not let this horrible experience define you.

***

A Message to the Unfaithful:

I really hope that you are reading this book for the right reason, because what's worse than betraying your partner in the first place is to betray them further by making insincere efforts to gain undeserved forgiveness and trust.

I am going to help you out from the get-go by giving you a chance to take a moment to be honest with yourself about your motivations behind taking this step. This is not just for the sake of your partner, but most importantly for your sake. I always tell my clients that no matter how good we are about lying to ourselves and others, and no matter how hard we try to bury those lies, they always find a way to float to the surface, much like scum floats over raw sewage.

So, what are the right motivations for somebody in your shoes to take this step?

One: Closure and Understanding

The truth of the matter is that you are the partner who is responsible for the devastating effects of the act of infidelity. We could sit here and argue about who started this chain reaction that led to the affair, as well as the circumstances that led you to making this decision, which we will delve into in later chapters, but, at this point, all of this will need to be on the back burner.

Regardless of the circumstances that lead to the affair and the potential outcome of this journey, you owe it to your partner and to yourself to take this opportunity to understand why this happened. Because what's worse than ending the relationship is ending it and walking away with the wrong conclusion of why it ended.

In other words, not having that closure and understanding will leave you and your partner with a blank void that can only be filled with assumptions, which are often not rooted in the reality of what took place. Sometimes, we opt for these assumptions, because it's better than a blank void.

***

Two: Healing and Rebuilding

Once you and your partner are able to successfully process the impact of infidelity as well as the circumstances that lead to such an act, the two of you will have an opportunity to rebuild your life and possibly your relationship. An affair is like a hurricane that wreaks havoc on the places it touches and leaves a trail of destruction. Before anyone can rebuild, the debris will have to be removed to start the new structures on a cleared foundation.

Now let's switch gears to the wrong motivations behind taking this step, which are many, however, they all fall under the category of ulterior motives, some of which are purely selfish and others are selfless, yet misguided.

Selfish motivations are any motivations that are driven by the need for protecting yourself from the negative emotional, physical, and economical consequences of ending the relationship (i.e. alimony, child custody, loss of financial support, not wanting to be alone, etc.).

Selfless, but misguided motivations are any motivations that are driven by protecting the greater good at the expense of yourself and your partner. In other words, these are the situations in which people try to save and rebuild a relationship for the wrong reasons even though it's not in the best interest of the couple. A classic example of this is, "We should stay together for the sake of the kids and avoid breaking up the family."

Now I am not saying that saving the family unit can't be a good motivation to rebuilding your relationship, but it cannot be the primary motivation; it's ok for it to be the bonus. If a couple decides to rebuild their relationship, they should do it because of their love to each other and their belief in their ability to make the necessary changes needed for creating and sustaining a happy and healthy relationship.

Now that we got the motivation talk out of the way, let's discuss your emotional state. A lot of people don't have much sympathy for the unfaithful due to the obvious fact that they made a conscious choice to put themselves in this situation. So, the next best thing to sympathy is empathy, which is an understanding of where you are coming from and the unpleasant feelings that you are experiencing as a result of your actions.

It's normal to experience shame, guilt, embarrassment, and anger toward yourself for making this mistake. Sometimes you will find yourself compelled to avoid dealing with your emotions because you can't fathom what will happen once that floodgate is open.

My advice to you is to fight against that pull and find the balance between experiencing those emotions and letting them take their natural course versus suppressing them and shutting them off completely out of the fear of being overwhelmed by them. You also want to avoid being stuck in the pity party of despair and shame, because, after all, once you fully experience the consequences of your behavior and learn the lessons from this experience, you will need to move forward in order to rebuild your life.

Lastly, I want to emphasize the significance of this step that you are taking with your partner toward healing from this affair. It's a rare opportunity that should not be squandered. In order for you to get the most out of it, you will need to push yourself out of your comfort zone to face some ugly truths. It will not be an easy process and with minimum guarantees for saving the relationship. But it's a journey on which you must embark in order to move forward.

***

Why Is It Important to Process Infidelity?

The main thing I hope you get from this book is to have the opportunity to understand what happened, why it happened, and where to go from here. The emotional impact of infidelity often paralyzes the mind and makes it difficult to think clearly and make wise decisions about what steps to take next. This is why processing infidelity is crucial to any efforts toward moving forward.

Failing to process infidelity robs you from the chance to learn from the mistakes that were made in this relationship which contributed to the affair. This is the point in which I emphasize the controversial fact that affairs are not the sole responsibility of the unfaithful, even though they are the ones who made the conscious choice of cheating.

This notion is very unpopular because, at face value, it can be seen as blaming the betrayed for the act of infidelity. But, I will tell you the same thing I tell all my clients: there is nothing that can justify, or excuse, acts of infidelity, but that doesn't mean that we should ignore the factors that paved the road for making this mistake possible.

Outlining those factors doesn't take the unfaithful off the hook for being responsible for their conscious actions; it simply provides an explanation for the inappropriate behavior versus sanctioning and excusing that behavior. Bottom line, the unfaithful and the betrayed both played a part in allowing the relationship to deteriorate to the critical point of infidelity. That responsibility ranges from acting inappropriately to fulfill real, or imagined, unmet needs to failing to recognize and address the warning signs that the relationship was in need of serious help.

So, what happens when couples fail to process infidelity? People end up making poor decisions. Here are the most common poor decisions caused by failing to process the acts of infidelity:

Running Away

The main motivation in this scenario is to avoid undertaking the hard and painful process of healing from infidelity. Some people will decide to end the relationship on the spot without fully processing what happened.

Ending the relationship on the spot by either the unfaithful or the betrayed can be appealing because it appeases your ego and prevents you from having to deal with some of the ugly and painful truths that brought you to this point. Running away also gives you the false sense of security that you are protecting yourself from the painful consequences of infidelity. The reason why this is a bad choice is because of the simple fact that avoiding to process the acts of infidelity is really just you putting blinders on to avoid seeing the serious problems that you need to fix within yourself in order for you to prevent finding yourself in a similar situation in the future, whether in this relationship or new ones. Not only that, but most importantly you could be missing out on the possibility of rebuilding your current relationship and making it even stronger than it was before. It's like opting to remove a salvageable molar instead of doing a necessary yet painful root canal to save it.

Cutting Corners

This is another common mistake. Here the unfaithful or the betrayed try to skip or rush certain steps of the healing process to minimize the pain and challenges associated with healing. A classic example of this is forgiving the unfaithful without understanding why they cheated and without seeing any proof of that person fixing the circumstances that led to the affair. Another example is minimizing the true impact of the act of infidelity to convince oneself and partner to sweep it under the rug to avoid taking responsibility and working to make the necessary changes to prevent future incidents. This is a poor choice because cutting corners does not fix the problem; it just provides a temporary band-aid that will assure that the contributing factors to the affair stay hidden yet active and unaddressed. It's like having a mold problem on your walls, and deciding to paint over it instead of scraping it off and treating your walls.

***

Doing Nothing

This decision is usually the byproduct of fear to act accompanied with the lack of knowledge on how to proceed. Here, one or both partners are aware of the infidelity and its impact on the relationship but are not sure how to proceed or are afraid to do something about it. So the main strategy in this option is the old idea of, "let's ignore it and hope it goes away." People find themselves at this juncture when they don't like the options in front of them that will allow them to deal with the problem. In other words, sometimes, when people are faced with equally difficult or unpleasant choices, they get stuck because they don't know which route to take because they don't like any of their options.

This may sound silly because you are probably wondering why people would do such an illogical thing. Well because it gives the illusion that not making a choice will delay the difficulties associated with those choices. What people are forgetting is the fact that avoiding to act does not guarantee that you avoid the consequence, even though it might delay it for a bit. Because, if you don't make a choice, things will deteriorate further to a point in which you won't even have the luxury of choosing one of those unpleasant options in front of you. So, wouldn't you rather be in control of your own destiny despite the lack of appeal in your choices? I know I would.

Chapter 2

Definition and Stats

"The saddest thing about betrayal is that it never comes from your enemies... It comes from Friends n loved ones."

--- Ash Sweeney

What Is Infidelity?

I am big on definitions because I believe it's the first building block in any attempt to examine, understand, and make sense of the things around us. In addition to that, laying out a concrete definition helps to draw clear lines between true acts of infidelity versus other problematic behaviors that impact couples which can manifest through acts of infidelity.

One of the main challenges of coming up with a single definition to the issue of infidelity is the fact that people come from various backgrounds and experiences, which contribute to having various ideas and definitions of what infidelity means for each person and each couple. The definition of infidelity not only differs from one member of the couple to the other but also differs from couple to couple based on what type of relationship lifestyle they adhere to.

An example of how the definition can vary within members of the same couple can be something along the lines of members of the same couple having different opinions on a particular "gray" behavior and whether or not it meets the threshold of infidelity such as the example of flirting with others or watching pornography.

Another example of how the definition of infidelity can differ from one couple to another can be seen in what type of relationship boundaries or lifestyle the couple adheres to. For example, the definition for a couple who practices an alternative lifestyle, such as swinging or polyamory, will have a different definition from another couple who practices traditional monogamy. This means that I had to come up with a definition that is flexible enough to accommodate the various world views of my clients without compromising the need of a clear, agreed upon framework for the concept of infidelity.

The definition I developed was created to take into consideration the different cultural, spiritual, and world views of my clients who happen to have different standards for relationships and expectations of one another. This is a definition that accommodates the individual needs and expectations of all couples regardless of their background.

This definition is built on my theoretical and clinical view of relationships as bonds that we seek to build with other people to

Ch. 2 Definition and Stats

27

fulfill emotional and physical needs. This premise dictates that such a bond lends itself to the same concept of any kind of partnership. When we commit to a relationship, there should be an agreed upon set of expectations that define what and how each one of our emotional and physical needs should be met by our partner. Any deviation or exception from that agreement without the consent of your partner constitutes an act of infidelity.

Simply put, infidelity is a conscious breach of a contract of exclusivity with your partner. It's engaging in *any* **need-fulfilling** behavior with other people other than your partner *without his or her consent.* I am talking about the behaviors that are motivated by the desire to fulfill emotional or physical needs that are supposed to be fulfilled exclusively by your partner based on the expressed and implied expectations that the two of you have of each other. This breach of contract manifests through having emotional, physical, and mixed affairs.

Types of Affairs

The specific type of needs driving the act of infidelity is what dictates the type of affair people have. Since there are two main categories of needs in all relationships, we can end up with three different types of affairs: physical, emotional and mixed. Keep in mind that due to our dual physical and emotional nature as human beings, we can never truly rule out an affair as purely physical or emotional, but the next best thing is to look for what was more of a primary drive.

Physical Affairs:

In this type of infidelity, the motivation behind the act is the fulfillment of unmet physical needs. In my clinical experience, I've noticed that this type of infidelity seems to be more prevalent with males than females. The attachment in those affairs is primarily physical, and the main goal is the fulfillment of sexual needs, desires, and fantasies. This can take the form of single or multiple one night stands or an ongoing arrangement with one or multiple sexual partners. Even though the motivations are physical, the unfaithful may experience the emotional benefit of feeling good about their ability to attract the physical attention of others as well as the satisfaction of fulfilling those needs.

Emotional Affairs:

Here the primary motivations behind the affairs are emotional. Based on my clinical experience, this type of affair is more prevalent with females than males. It usually starts when people are feeling unwanted and or desired by their partner. Not everyone starts emotional affairs with the intention of getting emotionally attached to someone else. A lot of the time, it starts with wanting to experience excitement through flirting which evolves into blurred boundaries. It's noteworthy to mention that emotional affairs often lead to physical affairs, even if the physical needs were not an issue that was lacking in the first place.

Mixed Affairs:

These types of affairs may have started primarily as physical or emotional, but went unchecked. In this scenario, the unfaithful's motivation behind the affair went beyond the fulfillment of unmet physical or emotional needs and they are now beginning to see the person they are cheating with as a surrogate for their partner or an idealized version of the relationship they want to have with their partner. Healing from those affairs can be more challenging due to the fact that, for all intents and purposes, we are dealing with two relationships: one that the unfaithful has with the betrayed and one that the unfaithful has with the person they are cheating with (the third party). One of these two relationships will have to end in order for the couple to move forward with their lives.

Infidelity and Mental Illness

Sometimes people commit infidelity for reasons other than what we discussed in the definition. The motivation for infidelity is not always due to the fulfillment of real or imagined unmet physical and emotional needs. In these scenarios, the motivations behind the act of infidelity are a symptom of a pathological condition that the unfaithful struggles with.

Understanding the motivation behind infidelity allows us to truly understand why infidelity happened in the first place. This will enable us to come up with the right solutions to fix those factors if we decide to proceed with rebuilding the relationship. We will also walk away with the right conclusion and closure if we decide that the relationship cannot be fixed.

There are many mental health disorders that have diagnostic symptoms that can manifest through the act of infidelity. The fact that infidelity in those situations is caused by the affliction of a mental disorder should not be used as an excuse to let the unfaithful off the hook for the choices they made. Because, after all, we should all be responsible for maintaining, monitoring, and treating our mental health. This is especially true, if we are aware of our symptoms and diagnosis. Having a mental health disorder does not mean that we are destined for a life without control, especially if we are diligent about seeking professional help from licensed psychiatrists and therapists. Determining whether or not the mental health issue contributed to the act of infidelity will simply allow us to come up with the best plan to understand and address the underlying factors that have contributed to the affair.

Here is a list of some of the common mental disorders that has one or more symptoms that can manifest through acts of infidelity. This list is not a comprehensive list and does not mean that everyone who has been diagnosed with these disorders has been unfaithful or will be any time in the near future. It simply means that some of the individuals who struggle with these disorders might have symptoms that could manifest through acts of infidelity. The symptoms criteria mentioned below is for informational purposes only and should not be used to diagnose yourself or your partner. This is a task that requires the expertise, training, and observation of licensed professionals. In other words, don't treat it like WebMD.

Bipolar I and II

In order to diagnose an individual with Bipolar I, they must experience at least one manic episode in addition to other criteria. In order to diagnose an individual with Bipolar II, they must experience at least one hypo manic episode in addition to other criteria.

There are many symptoms that need to be observed before determining that an individual is experiencing a manic episode or a hypomanic episode. The common features between manic and hypomanic episodes are two symptoms: one, "a distinct period of abnormally and persistently elevated, expansive or irritable mood;" and, two, "Excessive involvement in activities that have a high potential for painful consequences (e.g., engaging in unrestrained buying sprees, sexual indiscretions, or foolish business investments)."[1]

An individual with Bipolar I or II might be engaged in acts of infidelity due to the abnormal, elevated mood and excessive involvement in risky activities mentioned above. The inability to regulate mood and the impulsivity associated with it can create the right environment for impulsive, risky, poor choices.

Personality Disorders

These types of disorders are associated with the way a person thinks and feels about their self in relation to others and the world around them. Those ways of feeling and thinking are very pervasive and affect all different aspects of their interactions negatively and persistently. There are ten distinct types of personality disorders, but the ones that have the highest potential of symptoms manifesting through acts of infidelity are: Antisocial Personality Disorder, Borderline Personality Disorder, Histrionic Personality Disorder, and Narcissistic Personality Disorder.

Antisocial Personality Disorder

The hallmark of Antisocial Personality Disorder is the persistent pattern of disregard and violation of the rights of others.

---

[1] American Psychiatric Association: Diagnostic and Statistical Manual of Mental Disorders, Fifth Edition. Arlington, VA, American Psychiatric Association, 2013. Page 124

They fail to adhere to social norms and rules. They are deceitful and lie often to achieve personal gains. They are impulsive and recklessly disregard the safety of others. They lack remorse and empathy toward others regardless of how much pain they cause. [2]

A person with Antisocial Personality Disorder may have an affair simply because it's against social norms or because they feel like having multiple partners and don't care how this will affect their partner. Sometimes the motivation is simply to hurt their partner because of the fact that it's a pleasurable act for the antisocial.

Borderline Personality Disorder

The main feature of this disorder is the pattern of instability in self-image, relationships, affect, and impulse control. Individuals with this disorder have a pattern of unstable and intense relationships that swing between extreme idealization and devaluation. They are usually engaged in extreme efforts to avoid real or imagined abandonment. They have difficulties regulating their mood and usually display difficulties in controlling and expressing anger in appropriate ways.[3]

A person with Borderline Personality Disorder may have an affair out of anger at their partner or as a way to avoid real or imagined abandonment. Sometimes acts of infidelity are pursued to satisfy the chronic feeling of emptiness and to compensate for their negative self-image.

Histrionic Personality Disorder

The distinctive pattern in this disorder is attention seeking and excessive emotionality. Individuals with this disorder have this

---

[2] American Psychiatric Association: Diagnostic and Statistical Manual of Mental Disorders, Fifth Edition. Arlington, VA, American Psychiatric Association, 2013. Page 659.

[3] American Psychiatric Association: Diagnostic and Statistical Manual of Mental Disorders, Fifth Edition. Arlington, VA, American Psychiatric Association, 2013. Page 663

Ch. 2 Definition and Stats

urge to continuously be the center of attention. They use physical appearances to draw attention to self and often in inappropriate ways. Their interactions with others have poor boundaries that are often described as seductive, sexual, and flat out inappropriate. They are also easily influenced by others and consider relationships to be more intimate than they actually are. [4]

A person with this disorder might have an affair to get attention from their partner and others even though they are getting enough attention at home. Some have learned that the easiest way to get that attention is through provocative behavior and sexuality which is a recipe for a disaster in a monogamous relationship.

Narcissistic Personality Disorder

The main traits that characterize this disorder are feelings of grandiosity, the consistent need for admiration, and a lack of empathy to others. Individuals with this disorder are having an exaggerated sense of self-importance, specialness and uniqueness. This leads to a great sense of entitlement, in which they have high and unreasonable expectations of others and demand for preferential treatment. They are often preoccupied with fantasies of unlimited success, beauty, power or ideal love. They also are very exploitative and take advantage of others to achieve their goals. [5]

A person with Narcissistic Personality Disorder may engage in acts of infidelity to fulfill their unquenchable need for admiration by individuals other than their partner or simply because they believe that they are special and the rules of expected monogamy do not apply to them.

***

---

[4] American Psychiatric Association: Diagnostic and Statistical Manual of Mental Disorders, Fifth Edition. Arlington, VA, American Psychiatric Association, 2013. Page 667

[5] American Psychiatric Association: Diagnostic and Statistical Manual of Mental Disorders, Fifth Edition. Arlington, VA, American Psychiatric Association, 2013. Page 669

Infidelity and Sex Addiction

Sex addiction is not a diagnosable condition in the Diagnostic and Statistical Manual of Mental Disorders fifth edition (DSM-5). This publication is considered to be the clinician's Bible for diagnosing and treating mental disorders and it's developed by the American Psychiatric Association. The fact that sex addiction is not included in the DSM-5 is a reflection of how the field is divided on this issue. Some clinicians believe that such a phenomenon does not exist or if it did, there is no concrete and empirical way to categorize it and define it in a universal way that can be validated through research and clinical studies.

Others believe that sex addiction is a real phenomenon and its existence has been supported with many case studies and empirical data. They also believe that this phenomenon is just as destructive and devastating as other commonly accepted types of addictions that are currently included in the DSM-5.

I believe that the phenomenon of addiction is very real and has tangible effects on our lives. We are all susceptible to addiction to substances and behaviors. The main elements of addiction are impulsivity, loss of control, and obsession that often leads to destructive behaviors with consequences that cause significant amounts of personal and social distress.

To me, addiction does not take away the responsibility of the addict for the affair, but it provides me with insight on the contributing factors driving the acts of infidelity. In other words, it really helps me understand what needs to be fixed in the relationship and who is responsible for fixing it. This is not geared toward shifting the blame or responsibility exclusively to either the unfaithful or the betrayed, but is simply to help figure out who is responsible for what and to what extent that responsibility goes. Because, after all, even addictive behavior is driven by need. Once we identify that need, we can come up with a better, healthier way to fulfil that need so that we can be more successful in getting rid of the addictive behavior.

***

Infidelity and Sexual Identity

There are some instances in which the act of infidelity is caused by unclear or undeveloped sexual orientation identity. Here, the motivation behind the act is driven to fulfill physical needs or desires that cannot be fulfilled by the current partner due to their biological sex assignment. This can happen when the unfaithful is repressing their true sexual orientation which conflicts with the type of relationship he or she has with the current partner (i.e., repressing a homosexual or bisexual identity because he or she is in a heterosexual relationship or vise versa). In these scenarios, couples require an open discussion about their true sexual orientation and preferences and whether or not those orientations or preferences can be honored and fulfilled within the confines of this relationship without infringing on each other's sexual boundaries.

Infidelity Statistics and Facts

Infidelity is not a rare phenomenon. It's one of the most prevalent issues impacting marriages and committed relationships regardless of race, religion, cultural background, socioeconomic status, and sexual orientation. The reason I wrote this section is to show you some of the mind-blowing statistics about the true impact of this problem and our susceptibility to it. These numbers came from a recent study that was published in the Journal of Marital and Family Therapy. There are three main points that I want to convey to you through sharing this data.

Fact # 1: Infidelity Is More Common than You Think

- *In 41% of marriages, one or both spouses admit to infidelity, either physical or emotional.*
- *57% of men and 54% of women admit to committing infidelity in any relationship they've had.*

***

- *74% of men and 68% of women say that they would have an affair if they knew they would never get caught.*[6]

This is a large number of the population in which one or both partners have committed acts of infidelity or are actively thinking about it but not acting on it due to the fear of consequences. Keep in mind that this estimate might actually be higher due to people's tendency to not disclose such sensitive information.

This number shows that we are all susceptible to infidelity. This means that good people make bad choices, because the only other alternative explanation to this high number is that more than half of the population is a barrel of rotten apples, which is a very unlikely possibility. This number also proves that there are many people who are currently unsatisfied in their relationship, but find it easier to cheat instead of addressing and treating the individual and relationship problems that are contributing to their dissatisfaction.

It's noteworthy to mention that recent advances in technology have made it easier for people to cheat. Nowadays, we have social media, dating apps, and websites that are specifically designed for people who are unhappy in their relationships and looking for likeminded individuals who are interested in engaging in affairs. Keep in mind that infidelity should not be blamed on the advances in technology. The desire and motivation to cheat has always existed throughout the ages It's just that the new advances in technology make it easier to act on those impulses.

What Are Some of the Factors that Make Some People More Vulnerable and Susceptible to Infidelity?

The factors that make some people more susceptible to cheating reflect the actual causes and driving motivations behind the act of infidelity, which we will discuss in more detail in later

---

[6] Journal of Marital and Family Therapy. Associated Press. Infidelity Statistics. Internet. 01 Jan 2014. http://www.statisticbrain.com/infidelity-statistics/

chapters. The most common factor shared by all couples dealing with infidelity is the lack of mastery of one or more of the following skills: ability to asses needs of self and partner, ability to communicate effectively about those needs, ability to make necessary compromises to meet those needs, and the ability to adapt to life stressors and changes that may get in the way of meeting those needs. The lack of mastery in one or more of these skills is the cause of the majority of relationship problems. Keep in mind that observing the lack of these skills in you and your partner does not mean that an affair already took place; it simply means that you are at a high risk for inviting infidelity into your life.

Fact #2: A Large Number of Affairs Are Born in the Workplace

- *36% of men and women admit to having an affair with a co-worker.*
- *35% of men and women admit to infidelity on business trips.* [7]

It's very common for individuals to have affairs with co-workers. Think about it, we spend more time with co-workers than we do with our family. Not only is the quantity of time higher, but we also work with them in a team oriented environment in which we share certain responsibilities and tasks. The team environment often requires the development of a strong emotional bond since we are engaged in some sort of a professional partnership to perform our occupational duties. You hear people joke about the concept of a work spouse. That joke becomes a reality when people blur the lines of professional and emotional bonds. This is especially true when you have two individuals who are unsatisfied with their current relationship at home and have shared that dissatisfaction with one another. This allows the coworkers to over identify with each other's struggles which, in return, causes them

---

[7] Journal of Marital and Family Therapy. Associated Press. Infidelity Statistics. Internet. 01 Jan 2014. http://www.statisticbrain.com/infidelity-statistics/

to play the nurturing, supportive role that should be exclusively reserved for their spouse. This leads to a situation in which the co-worker becomes a surrogate spouse. Furthermore, having a job that requires travel on business trips makes it easier and more tempting for individuals to cross those boundaries with their co-workers or seek affairs in faraway places without raising suspicion of the partner who assumes that the unfaithful is working.

What Occupations Increase the Risk Factors for Acts of Infidelity?

I work with hundreds of couples from all walks of life who come from different occupational backgrounds and environments ranging from a stay-at-home partner to high-level corporate executives, and everything in between. The truth is each occupation has its own set of stressors that may increase the potential for creating the right environment for infidelity. So instead of focusing on particular jobs, I will focus on the occupational hazards that these jobs have in common based on how it negatively impacts the quality of our relationships.

The High Demands Hazard

High demand occupations take many forms, but think of it in terms of how the job duties of that occupation affects you and your partner's ability to have adequate time and adequate mental and physical energy needed for sustaining a healthy, satisfying relationship.

Some of the high demands take the form of long or strange hours that limit the availability of time needed to spend with your partner. This can be long shifts, overtime, graveyard shifts, frequent travel, bringing work home, or working weekends and holidays. The more time you spend at work, the less time you have to spend with your partner and on your relationship.

Another form of high demand can be seen in the amount of mental energy needed to perform job duties successfully. Some jobs are so mentally draining that they cause you and your partner to be mentally depleted by the time you get home to be available

     Ch. 2 Definition and Stats

for any kind of necessary emotional interaction. Some jobs are emotionally taxing because there is close to zero tolerance for making mistakes due to what could be at stake as a result of poor performance. Other jobs are emotionally taxing because of the nature of the things we are exposed to during our job duties and whether or not we have a tough enough skin to prevent traumatization.

As far as physical energy, some jobs require a tremendous amount of energy and stamina in order to perform the tasks successfully. Having a job that is physically demanding impacts your day-to-day interaction with your partner, because, let's face it, if you are dog tired by the end of the day, the only thing that you are thinking about is decompressing and recharging your batteries, which often means shutting everything down and focusing on whatever self-centered activities can help you unwind, which may or may not include spending quality time with your partner. Physically demanding jobs also have accumulative affects that usually manifest through the development of chronic medical conditions that adds another layer of limitation to our abilities to spend quality time with our partners.

The Work Culture Hazard

Regardless of the type of industry, every work environment has the potential of being a cesspool of inappropriate interactions. But there are certain types of jobs and industries in which blurred boundaries and inappropriate interactions with clients, supervisors, and co-workers are some of the tools needed to be successful in achieving occupational quotas or getting advancement opportunities. Some of these jobs have a need for wining and dining or flirting which is usually packaged as "Good Customer Service Skills needed to gain new customers." In other jobs, climbing up requires a quid pro quo interaction to earn advancement opportunities. This type of culture exists in highly competitive and profit-driven industries in which the main goal is to make a profit at any cost despite the ethical and moral conduct. Other environments have that culture simply because of the nature of the product that they offer; think along the lines of the adult entertainment industry.

Fact #3: Many Couples Are Able to Survive Infidelity and Manage to Rebuild Their Relationship

- *31% of marriages last after an affair has been admitted to or discovered[8]*

This is a very optimistic number, especially when considering that infidelity is one of the most hurtful acts one can commit in a relationship. What is impressive about this number is if you ask anyone on the street whether or not they can forgive acts of infidelity, you will find an overwhelming majority say no. This mirrors what I often hear my clients say: "I never thought that I would consider forgiving anyone who cheats on me, but now that it happened, I am not sure anymore." This uncertainty is not a reflection of weakness or lack of respect to self; it's a reflection of the fact that relationships cannot be defined by single acts of selfishness, regardless of the ugliness of those acts. The truth of the matter is that despite the pain experienced by the betrayed, sometimes they are able to see the goodness of their partner and are able to remember a time when the relationship was amazing before it was tainted by the act of infidelity. This is especially true if the relationship had a strong foundation prior to the onset of the factors that created the right environment for the affair.

What Are the Factors that Allow People to Recover from Infidelity?

Even though one out of three couples is able to survive and heal from infidelity, it does not mean that it's an easy and painless process. The couples who are most likely to succeed in this journey must have the crucial ingredient of a high relationship-net-

---

[8] Journal of Marital and Family Therapy. Associated Press. Infidelity Statistics. Internet. 01 Jan 2014. http://www.statisticbrain.com/infidelity-statistics/

worth. It's like *Kelly's Bluebook*. If you get in a car wreck, you are presented with two options: repair the car or total it. That decision will be based on what the actual value of the car is in relation to what it's going to cost you to fix it. If your car was a car that you really loved and were very satisfied with at some point in time prior to the accident, then you are more likely to spend the time and effort needed to fix it and restore it to be even better than it was prior to the accident. Couples who had a good foundation at some point in their relationship prior to the affair are more likely to be successful in surviving this journey, because they are invested in the process and the relationship is worthy of all the pain and energy needed to heal it.

In addition to having a high relationship-net-worth, the couple needs to possess certain qualities that would allow them to withstand the many challenges associated with this difficult process, such as the abilities to be patient, honest, emotionally resilient, and dedicated to the process of healing.

Chapter 3

Causes of Infidelity

"Love is a feeling, marriage is a contract, and relationships are work."

--- Lori Gordin

Why Does Infidelity Happen?

In the previous chapter, we discussed the definition of infidelity as well as the different types of affairs. Infidelity is just like any other human behavior in the sense that it's motivated to fulfill particular needs. Those needs can be physical, emotional, or a mixture of both.

Everything we do is driven to fulfill what we perceive as necessary physical and emotional needs which must be met in order to, not only survive life, but also to enjoy it. This is one of the driving factors that compel people to seek and establish any kind of relationship. Even though a lot of us can survive by relying on ourselves to fulfill our emotional and physical needs, there comes a point in which some of our needs cannot be met without having a relationship with another human being, especially when it comes to emotional needs like the need to be loved and desired by someone else.

Can we survive without partnering with others through relationships? Sure, but *survive* is the keyword, which means we are talking about quality of life. We all have the ability go through life without having to resort to being in a relationship, but life is a lot better and far more fulfilling if we are able to share our lives with others.

Affairs, in all the various types, are a form of relationship we use to fulfill our emotional and physical needs. They are different from the type of committed relationship you have with your partner in two main aspects: legitimacy and authenticity.

Legitimacy (Rightfulness)

I want you think back about the concept of relationships as business partnerships. In order for the partnership to succeed, each partner must commit to a contract that outlines the number of partners in the relationship, rights and duties of each partner toward each other, and an outline of the expected emotional and physical needs that must be met through the partnership. Once you and your partner commit to this agreement, all of your efforts and attempts to fulfill your emotional and physical needs will be considered legitimate and sanctioned as long as you are operating within the agreed upon parameters.

When people get involved in affairs, they start another agreement on the side with other partners for the purpose of fulfilling some or all of the needs that they previously agreed to meet exclusively with the partner in the first agreement. This fact makes the second agreement illegitimate and any attempts to fulfill any needs under this new contract becomes invalid.

Authenticity (Realness)

Affairs are appealing and addicting despite the negative consequences and turmoil people experience during the affair and in the aftermath, because they offer a quick and easy fix for fulfilling our needs in a way that exceeds the expectations in a normal relationship. It's sort of like the difference between getting high on life versus high on crack. The first requires efforts that will pay off gradually in a non-exaggerated way. The second is immediate, effortless, and over the top.

What gives affairs this magical ability is the fact that they are one dimensional types of relationships in which the contract is built on fulfilling one or a few very specific needs with minimum risk, investment, and obligation for both parties. This makes the fulfillment of these needs easier and grander. People enjoy affairs because it allows them to play out an unrealistic version of a relationship in which you get to have all the fun, but without the work. In other words, it's a lot easier to have great sex and affection in an affair simply because that is all the relationship is built on. Meaning you are not worried about real-life issues like co-parenting, financial planning, and the endless list of chores and responsibilities that regular couples have to deal with.

When needs are not being fulfilled in a committed relationship, the right thing to do is to figure out what needs are not being met and what barriers are preventing those needs from being met. This translates into a lot of soul searching to figure out what's missing, why it's missing and what needs to be done to fix it. The person whose needs are not being met, as well as their partner who is supposed to be fulfilling these needs, will have to make some major changes to fix this problem. This process usually takes time and effort in order to achieve the desired results.

Affairs, on the other hand, are types of relationships that are less complicated in the sense that they allow us to design them in a way that gives us what we need at a price we are willing to pay for fulfilling these needs. In other words, the person who feels that their needs are not being met in the current committed relationship finds the option of an affair easier because they get to choose what type of involvement they want to have with the other person in the affair.

Different Types of Causes

The idea that infidelity is a breach of contract of exclusivity sets the stage for allowing us to begin to categorize the many different causes which compel people to seek affairs. This means that we have to ask the important question of why people breach their contracts of exclusivity. There are three main reasons—one: never had a clear contract in the first place; two: have a contract, but one or both is not fulfilling their part; and three: the agreed upon contract terms are not meeting the needs of one or both partners.

One: Never Established a Clear, Agreed Upon Contract in the First Place

The majority of the couples I work with are often surprised when they hear about the concept of a contract that outlines rights and expectations in a committed relationship. This is because most of us grow up with no clear guidelines or instructions on what a healthy relationship looks like. Here are the two most common factors that prevent couples from establishing this clear contract:

Failing to Identify and Clearly Define Needs

A lot of us are not in touch with our own needs because we never acquired that skill. Most of us have an awareness that something is missing, but we are unable to clearly define what it is. This is especially true when it comes to emotional needs. Most of the time, you hear people say things like, "I am not really happy," which is a general statement that doesn't really identify concrete needs that are not being fulfilled. So, if we don't know what is causing the "unhappiness" how are we going to expect our partner to fulfill this unknown need?

Sometimes needs are poorly defined or mixed up which is almost as bad as unidentified needs. In these situations, we mix up two distinct needs because they happen to correlate with one another. This mix up sets the stage for our partners to fail because we are presenting them with confusing and unclear messages. For example, the need to feel loved and the need to be sexually desired are two distinct needs that correlate with one another. But each one has a specific set of actions that needs to be fulfilled. Failure and success in one arena should not automatically cause similar results in the other. In other words, failing to fulfill the needs of being sexually desired by your partner should not automatically be assumed as a failure in his or her ability to make you feel loved, because sex is one way of expressing love rather than the only way.

Failing to Agree to Clearly Defined Needs

Being able to get in touch with our needs and clearly define them in concrete ways is the first step toward establishing a relationship contract. The second step in this process is reaching an agreement with your partner about those needs and the actions needed to fulfill them. This is the part that a lot of couples get stuck in without ever reaching a resolution. One of the most common barriers in this step is the inability to compromise, which can be caused by a variety of reasons such as lack of compatibility and unrealistic expectations.

There is no rule that says in order for people to have successful relationships they have to be a carbon copy of one another. As a matter of fact, the differences between us and our partners are often the basis for attraction as well as the benefit for being with someone who has different experiences and world views, which can allow you to grow as a person and learn from one another.

Even though differences are healthy and enriching, they can be harmful if they are extreme. Every relationship requires a compromise, which I define as meeting in the middle for the right reasons without having to change the core identity of who you are as an individual (assuming that your core is good and positive). But, if the worldview and differences between you and your partner are too extreme, then there is no room for a compromise, because the only way for the two of you to come to an agreement is by one of you having to deny your true self, which is difficult to do without any resentment. For example, a monogamist and a polygamist can never really reach a compromise because they are fundamentally different and have very opposing views that cannot be mediated without having one of them compromise the integrity of their identity.

Sometimes, couples are unable to reach an agreed upon contract because one or both have unrealistic expectations for their needs. This usually stems from a vastly skewed perception of what is feasible, normal, and conducive to healthy functioning. Here, we have a scenario in which a specific need is being identified and clearly defined, but the actions necessary to fulfill these needs are unrealistic in general or particularly because of the limitations of our partner's interests, abilities, and worldviews. This makes the clearly defined expectation unachievable, despite our best efforts, leaving us unfulfilled.

Two: Have a Contract, but One or Both is Not Fulfilling Their Part.

Some of the couples I work with have managed to establish a clear, realistic, and agreed upon contract, yet they still ended up in the infidelity trap. So, how do they end up in the same place as the couple who didn't even establish a contract? The answer is very simple. A good contract should be adaptive and flexible to accommodate the changes that couples undergo as well as the different life stressors they face. In these scenarios, couples fail when they expect to have the original contract remain unchanged despite the passage of time, which often brings forth many new variables that need to be accounted for in the dynamic of the relationship. There are three main factors that can contribute to this scenario: failing to adapt to life stressors, getting overwhelmed with responsibilities, and failing to evaluate and address changes in needs.

Failing to Adapt to Life Stressors

Whether you are single or in a relationship, life will always present you with some challenges and stressors. Some of those challenges can be negative, such as illness or job loss, or they can be positive, like having a baby or a job promotion. Life stressors require us to adapt. This adaptation is easier when you are single because you get to choose what changes you are willing to make to accommodate the new life stressor. When you are in a relationship, however, this task becomes more complicated because now you and your partner have to agree on how to adapt to the new life stressors in a way that still fulfills your physical and emotional needs.

What usually happens is that a life stressor takes place and each partner adapts to it differently without conscious thought or effort of communication about the new changes. Most likely, the adaptations made by each partner in this situation are one-sided and only take into consideration the interests of the individual, or the adaptations are misguided in the sense that each partner is making assumptions about what the other person is going to be comfortable with.

Classic example, the sex life of a couple changes dramatically after having a baby, simply due to the fact that now the couple is using the resource of energy and time to spend on another human being. Add to it the hormonal changes as well as the adjustment to being a parent and you have a drastic decline in the quality and quantity of sexual activities.

Here is a situation in which a new life stressor of having a baby is introduced and the couple misses an opportunity to renegotiate how they are going to fulfill each other's emotional and physical needs under the new life changing event. Obviously, their sex life can't be exactly the same as it was before the baby, (at least not for a while) but that doesn't mean that it has to stop completely. What needs to happen here is for the couple to have a healthy discussion about new ways for fulfilling those needs that accommodates the new life stressors. What happens instead are extreme changes on one partner's end without any discussion or agreement about those changes. This leaves a lot of room for misinterpretation of intentions and resentment about unmet needs. A healthy need contract is one that takes into consideration the introduction of life stressors which warrants open dialogue about renegotiating new ways to fulfill each other's needs.

Getting Overwhelmed with Responsibilities

Another common factor that prevents couples from meeting the expectations they agreed to in their contract is being overwhelmed with life responsibilities. We all struggle with balancing the different roles we play in life as workers, parents, spouses, friends, family members, etc. Sometimes we have so much on our plate that we fall short in meeting our partner's expectations. In these scenarios, one or both partners allow life to get in the way of meeting the relationship expectations. Sometimes there is just too much to handle and we need help. Other times we are mismanaging our time and not balancing our priorities. There are usually a lot of excuses made for why the relationship needs are taking a back seat. What I tell everyone is that the satisfaction in our relationship is one of the most crucial areas in life that requires our constant attention, because if we are not happy with our partner, everything else suffers.

Once again, communication is key, because it's unrealistic to expect that we are always going to be achieving 100% accuracy in all aspects of our life. It's ok to fall short on some of our relationship expectations at times as longs as there is a valid reason and that reason is communicated to our partner, and we are actively working together to correct this situation to get back on track again. But what usually happens is that we get behind on our commitment and somehow expect that our partners will understand and not have any hard feelings or ask any other questions. This is one of the reasons people end up resenting each other, because, in addition to their needs not being met, they are also receiving the message that their needs are a low priority.

Failing to Evaluate and Address Changes in Needs

We all undergo many changes through our lifespan. Changes are caused by life events that continue to shape who we are and how we perceive the world around us. We also experience physical and emotional changes as we age. Our needs evolve and grow as we grow. This means some priorities get shifted, some new needs arise and others fade away or take a backseat. Those changes in needs should have a proper adjustment in our expectations contract with our significant others in order for our partnerships to continue to be fulfilling for everyone involved.

Even with the needs that remain constant throughout the lifespan of the relationship, the currency and actions required to fulfill those needs may have to change and take a different form based on where we are in life and the situations we are in. For example, the need to be supported emotionally by our partner can take the passive form of listening and providing encouragement when we are day dreaming about future plans, or it can shift to an active form of providing solutions and taking charge of responsibilities when we are dealing with a chronic aliment or a major negative life stressor.

One of the most common mistakes couples make is failing to recognize those changes in need in themselves and in their partner, which leads to a lot of wasted efforts in which one or both think that they are fulfilling their end of the deal in the relationship, because they are following the original contract. In other words, everyone is carrying on with business as usual, but somehow the same efforts that worked all this time are no longer satisfactory, which causes a lot of resentment and frustration for both partners.

A lot of couples are on auto pilot and often clueless about this change. Other couples have some sort of awareness of the fact that what used to work before is no longer working. These couples make the second biggest mistake of attributing the dissatisfaction as a normal rut of a long-term relationship. What they should've been doing instead is revisiting the original contract and reevaluating their needs and renegotiating the new ways to meet those needs.

This a good time to debunk a common myth that a lot of people have about relationships, which is the notion that all relationships must experience ruts as part of the normal wear and tear of being together for a long time and being overwhelmed with life responsibilities. My biggest problem with this notion is that it sets the stage for accepting a decline in the quality of the relationship simply because of the passage of time. This lets people off the hook from being held accountable to the part they played in the decline of quality. It's true that keeping up with relationship expectations becomes more challenging the longer couples are together. The longer you are together, the more you are presented with life challenges and responsibilities. However, that doesn't mean the quality of the relationship should decline, especially if the couple is successfully addressing these challenges as a team and readjusting their expectations of one another in ways that take into consideration the impact of those challenges on their lives.

There are some scenarios in which couples are aware of the changes in needs as well as the necessity for making the adjustments required to accommodate those changes, but they make the fatal mistake of making assumptions about what those changes are without communicating with one another, which leads to more wasted efforts.

It's important for couples to understand each other's needs and anticipate what will work for them when it comes to meeting those needs, but sometimes we become prisoners of our own narrow views about what is required to fix a problem. It goes something like this, "I know that he/she is not happy about this situation, so here is what I will do to fix it:_____, because, if I was in his/her shoes, that's what I would want to happen." At face value, we can accept that this action is coming from a good place of wanting to anticipate needs and taking actions to make our partners happy. The only problem with this is that when we are engaged in this kind of thinking, we usually end up choosing the actions that are convenient for us to do versus what our partner is expecting us to do to fix the problem. Most of the time, this requires significant effort and change on our part. I am not saying that whatever is chosen during those scenarios is off the mark every time, but what I know for sure is that it robs your partner from weighing in on whether or not the changes you are planning to make are going to fix the problem.

Three: The Agreed Upon Contract Terms Have Never Met the Needs of One or Both Partners.

This is one of the most frustrating scenarios of infidelity that couples struggle with. The frustration comes from the fact that it's difficult for the betrayed to understand why the unfaithful acted against the terms that he or she agreed to, especially when the betrayed held up their end of the deal. What adds insult to injury is the fact that the betrayed is taking all the right steps needed to start the relationship on the right track by clearly communicating their expectations from the onset as well as communicating the changes in expectation, yet they still find themselves in this unfair situation, despite the fact that the unfaithful had ample opportunity to say, "No thanks. I can't accept these terms." So how the heck does this happen? This is entirely driven by the unfaithful's intentions as well as their assessment of their own ability prior to signing off on the relationship contract. This creates two situations. In the first, the unfaithful was never willing to follow through with the agreement. In the second, the unfaithful was willing to follow through, but was unable to do so.

Was Never Willing in the First Place

As much as I believe in the notion that people are inherently good, I also believe that people are inherently selfish. Most of us learn that the best way to live a healthy life is through cooperation and compromise, allowing us to meet our needs and the needs of others, especially those we care about. Some of us, on the other hand, never learned this lesson because we were either never put in a situation in which we had to be forced to not lead a life of selfishness, or because despite our awareness of our interdependence on one another, we still try to find a way to beat the system.

The way this plays out in relationships is that you have individuals who are seeking relationships for the sole purpose of satisfying their own needs and desires, without any intentions for reciprocation. These individuals are self-centered and do not care about the desires and needs of their partners. This changes the dynamic of the relationship from a partnership in which both parties have equal rights and responsibilities to a parasite/host dynamic in which one party is simply using the other to fulfill its own selfish needs. These individuals are often aware of their own selfish intentions, but find creative ways to hide that agenda. They usually give the appearance of caring about their partner's needs. They accomplish this by doing just enough to maintain the facade, as long as such efforts don't get in the way of their own needs.

The driving force behind the actions here is selfishness and the desire to have your cake and eat it, too. The general idea here is that the unfaithful will go along with the expectations that don't conflict with what they want, but will disregard the expectations that conflict with what they want. The game plan is for the unfaithful to get what they want in secret or hope that the betrayed will change their view on their expectations of the relationship's exclusivity.

Was Willing but Not Able

Being honest with ourselves and who we are and what we are capable of can be tricky at times. I work with many couples in which the main cause of relationship conflict was a poor assessment of one's abilities. There is nothing wrong with aspiring to change certain aspects of ourselves for the purpose of achieving growth and healthy functioning. However, such change should not be at the cost of our partners who know what they want and what they are capable of and make the same assumption about us and our ability to fulfill the contract of exclusivity that we agreed to sign.

A lot of people commit to relationships and agree to the contract of exclusivity without putting too much thought on their own ability to do what it takes to honor their part of the deal. Sometimes it's a wishful thinking type of situation in which people assume they are going to be capable of exclusivity, even though they have never been put in a situation that requires such a commitment. Here you have a lot of good intentions, but poor assessment of one's abilities and readiness for a committed relationship.

This is why it's crucial for everyone seeking relationships to spend a lot of time identifying what they are hoping to get out of the relationship, what they are willing to give back, and whether or not they are ready to make that commitment. This will safeguard against many unnecessary hurts and heartaches.

Identifying the specific scenario that led to the breach of your contract of exclusivity is not going to make the act of infidelity less painful or easier to heal from. Knowing the exact cause will simply help you to assess your chances of healing from the affair. It does so by allowing you to determine whether or not you are able and willing to fix the underlying factors that have caused the affair. My advice to you is to take the time to figure which one of the scenarios mentioned above best describes your situation. Be honest with yourself and your partner during this process. Failing to do so will lead to moving forward in the wrong direction.

PART II

Healing from Infidelity

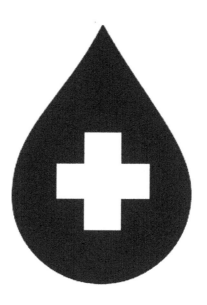

Chapter 4

The First Milestone: Setting the Stage for Healing

"By failing to prepare, you are preparing to fail."

---Benjamin Franklin

Step 1: Making a Conscious Choice

Now that we have covered the definition of infidelity and the main causes of it, it's time for you to take a very important step that will impact the rest of your life. The step I am talking about is making the conscious choice to heal from this awful experience. The reason I need you to make a conscious decision to take this step, versus agreeing to take this step because it is what you are supposed to do, is because it will be one of the most difficult things you will undertake, whether you are the betrayed or the unfaithful.

The journey of healing can be long and treacherous, filled with many challenges and hardships, but it's a journey you can't afford to avoid. Doing so will guarantee failure in this current relationship as well as many challenges in future relationships. It's like healing a broken bone; you can either do it properly by taking the inconvenient measures of wearing a cast and going through physical therapy to regain healthy functioning, or choose not to do anything, which leads to a best-case scenario of a poorly mended bone that can't function properly and causes chronic pain.

What makes this journey difficult is the enormous amount of emotional pain that must be processed and endured in order to heal. You also need to consider all the behavioral changes that should have taken place prior to the affair to have a satisfying relationship. Now, making behavioral changes is hard enough in regular circumstances, but can be ten times more challenging when it's done under difficult emotional circumstances such as the ones that are present during infidelity. This is why successfully completing the healing process will help couples survive future relationship conflicts.

An additional twist to this hardship is the fact that completing this journey does not ensure that you and your partner will be able save your relationship and make it better than it used to be. This means that you are being asked to do a lot of hard work with no guarantees of saving your relationship. You might be asking, "Then why the heck would I put myself through this?" Fair question. This is the part in which it is important to make the significant distinction of what types of healing you can expect from this journey: healing as a couple and healing as an individual.

Healing as a couple is the happy ending that most aspire to achieve. The way this story ends is with both partners learning more about themselves and each other and making the necessary changes they should have made prior to the affair. They also walk away with a new understanding of each other's needs and expectations as well as the tools and skills required to help them successfully assess and address each other's needs going forward.

Healing solo is a possibility that both you and your partner should be prepared for. The way this story ends is with one or both partners walking away with a clear understanding of why the affair happened and which part each person played in contributing to the circumstances that led to it. The healing benefit in this scenario comes from closure and a clear understanding of what really took place versus false assumptions about what happened. This will give the couple an opportunity to learn from the mistakes they made and identify the skills they need to be successful in future relationships.

Both types of healing require the same crucial ingredients, which are processing the affair, understanding why it happened, and owning up to the parts played in creating the circumstances that led to it. The type of ending you will get out of this journey is determined by three different factors: compatibility, readiness for commitment, and willingness to give it a chance.

Compatibility

Sometimes couples find out that the main cause of dissatisfaction in the relationship is a lack of compatibility from the onset of the relationship, which will always leave the couple dissatisfied with one another, regardless of their best efforts to compromise. This leads to having affairs with others who seem to be more suitable and compatible partners, at face value. There are many reasons why we establish relationships with others who we are not compatible with, such as unplanned pregnancy, socioeconomic pressures, poor understating of our own needs and desires, etc. The journey to heal from infidelity provides couples with the unique opportunity to evaluate their compatibility with one another and to discover to what degree it affects their satisfaction with the relationship. Couples who are not compatible will come to the conclusion that their happily ever after can only be achieved with someone who is more compatible with them.

Readiness for Commitment

In some cases, the unfaithful might find out that he or she was never ready to commit to exclusivity in the first place. Other times, the unfaithful might have been ready to commit at the onset of the relationship, but now he/she feels that they might be happier if they were not committed to an exclusive relationship and would like to continue living that way. The logical course of action here is to avoid setting up the couple for failure by having one partner who is ready to commit take a risk on somebody who is not ready or willing to commit to exclusivity. In order for couples to succeed in rebuilding trust, both have to be ready to make that commitment to themselves and each other.

Willingness to Give It a Chance

This is one of main barriers that prevents couples from healing together. The unwillingness to give the unfaithful a chance can be caused by a variety of reasons, but the common theme is pride and fear. Affairs are one of the most disrespectful acts a person can commit in a relationship, and they are damaging to our egos. The main struggle here is how to give the unfaithful a chance without feeling like a doormat. When the betrayed fails to resolve that struggle, they choose ego and pride, which leads to ending the relationship. Another chance can be either weakness or strength depending on your motivations for choosing that route in the first place. In other words, couples need to be honest with themselves about their motivations for giving and accepting another chance. This is a tough thing to assess for most people, so the golden rule is as follows: good motivations are born out of true love and care for the other person and the realization that there is more good than bad in the relationship as well as a belief in each other's ability to make changes. Bad motivations are anything that stems from secondary issues like fear of being alone, finances, impact of divorce, and so on.

The fear aspect of giving another chance comes from the need to protect ourselves from future harm. The sources of this fear include doubts about our own ability to make and stick to the changes needed for this relationship to work, as well as the fear of not being able to overcome the affair. The betrayed worries that he or she may not be able to forgive the unfaithful, and the unfaithful worries that the betrayed will never be able to get past the affair. Both fears are valid. However, doubts about each other's abilities can be dispelled. The couple must identify what they need to change and agree to give each other a chance to attempt to make those changes to see whether or not those doubts are well-founded. As far as the fear of failing to forgive, couples must accept the fact that granting forgiveness in this early stage is unrealistic and therefore seems unattainable, especially when there is no evidence of the unfaithful's ability to make and sustain changes. However, forgiveness can be seen as a more attainable goal if the couple focuses on making the necessary changes to earn trust which will eventually pave the road to gaining forgiveness.

Step 2: Agreeing on the Logistics

Despite the overwhelming emotions that the two of you are experiencing, it's important to agree on some of the concrete logistics that need to be discussed in order to create the best environment for healing. I am talking about the basic questions of "where," "who," "when," and "how" that the two of you need to agree on prior to proceeding further in the process.

Living Together or Separately

Let's start with the "where." A lot of couples are not sure on whether or not they should stay in the same house or live separately while they are healing from the affair. My recommendation is for the couple to be living in the same household as long as they are not explosive toward one another physically or emotionally and are able to give each other space when needed. I recommend being in the same household for three main reasons—one: when people are apart, it's easier to make wrong assumptions about each other's feelings, intentions, and behaviors; two: living under the same roof will allow both partners to process the impact of the trauma together, which facilitates the expression of feelings; and three: living together will give the couple the opportunity to demonstrate their ability to make and sustain positive changes.

Minimizing Outsider Influence

As far as the "who" is concerned, a couple should make a decision on who should be privy to the details of their affair. My recommendation is always to keep it between the couple and the professional venues they seek to help them process the affair. The reason why it should be kept private is because when we involve other people in our business, we also solicit their bias. In other words, people usually reach out during rough times to other people who they feel close to, such as family members and friends. Each one of these people has their own biases and opinions which may guide the support and advice they provide to you.

Furthermore, those individuals will form their own opinion about your partner which will stay with them regardless of whether or not you decide to stay or leave the relationship. Whoever you reach out to now will have a one-sided perception of your partner which might never go away if the two of you decide to stay together. Excluding others from the details of the affair is easier said than done, because, let's face it, it's difficult to hide the impact of affairs on our wellbeing from others. So, my advice is, if people ask, simply give the following statement, "We are having marriage problems, and we are working on it." If you and your partner have already involved others in your affair, my advice is to keep future details private and give the simple statement of, "We are trying to work things out."

The Third Party Involvement

This is the part where we should introduce the person with whom the unfaithful had the affair. I chose the term of "the third party," because it's a neutral term that can be applicable for all the different types of circumstances surrounding the affair. This is based on the fact that not all of the unfaithful's affair partners are always aware of the unfaithful's preexisting commitment.

Here we have two scenarios: one in which the unfaithful already ended the affair and has said what they needed to say to the third party in order to keep that door closed forever; or, the door to that third party has not been closed yet for a variety of reasons that we will uncover later on. What's important at this point is that the unfaithful agrees to end all communication of all forms with the third party while working on healing from the affair. This is especially true if the unfaithful is honest with themselves about their intention to figure out whether or not they can save their current relationship. It's like I tell all of my clients, "you can't have one foot in and one foot out. You have to pick a lane so that you can see it through to the end to figure out if this is where you want to be."

If the door has not been shut already, the unfaithful needs to tell the third party that they are currently working on their marriage and are not interested in future communications. This can be tricky if the third party happens to be a co-worker or someone who is difficult to avoid because of social circumstances. Here, the couple has to come up with creative ways to stop future contact, even if it requires finding another job or choosing a different worksite. It's also crucial that the betrayed is informed of any attempts of the third party to try to connect with the unfaithful. This will show transparency and give the couple a chance to decide on how to handle those attempts.

Step 3: Anticipating and Preparing for Challenges

Despite the conscious choice to heal from infidelity and the agreement on the logistics, couples will face a variety of challenges that can only be conquered through clarifying your expectations with one another while the two of you are working on healing. Think of it as setting the ground rules of interaction during this highly emotional and sensitive time in which every word and gesture counts and can negatively influence and skew this whole process.

***

The Challenge of Honesty about Feelings and Expectations

It's vital that the two of you are honest with yourselves and with each other about your feelings and expectations. After the affair, couples experience new feelings and expectations that they haven't encountered before. A lot of these feelings and expectations are not conducive to healthy functioning.

For example, a common feeling the betrayed will experience is insecurity. Now, illegitimate feelings of insecurity are damaging in a healthy relationship. But, insecurity as a result of an affair is a legitimate feeling under the current circumstances, because the unfaithful did actually go to someone else to fulfill his or her needs. Despite the legitimacy of this feeling, it's still something uncomfortable to experience, especially if the betrayed never had to experience this feeling prior to the affair.

In order for the betrayed to manage and process the feeling of insecurity, he or she will need to have reassurance from the unfaithful. This reassurance can take many forms, but it has to be in a form that is healthy and conducive to healing as well as in a currency that the betrayed understands and accepts as an act of reassurance.

Now, imagine if the betrayed was not honest with his/herself about having those feelings of insecurity or if they were able to admit it to themselves but were ashamed to share it with their partner. What would happen? Well, the feeling of insecurity is not going to go away unless the betrayed expresses the need for reassurance. What usually happens is that the betrayed suppresses this feeling as well as the expectation for needing reassurance, however, they expect the unfaithful to provide the reassurances even though that need was not expressed. That lack of fulfillment of that need will impede the healing process and reaffirm to the betrayed the belief that the unfaithful does not care about healing which will set this whole process up for failure.

Think of it this way, regardless of how comfortable each of you are about the feelings you are experiencing and the expectations attached to those feelings, you are not going to be able to do something with those feelings without taking the first step of admitting to having them and making the second step of sharing them with your partner. Doing so will give the two of you an opportunity to examine those feelings and make a determination on whether or not they are appropriate for the circumstances. In addition, when the two of you come to the conclusion that those feelings are appropriate, you will be able to agree on the best actions to take to manage those feelings effectively.

Using the previous example, sometimes couples are able to admit to and share a legitimate feeling of insecurity, but may have an unhealthy expectation of how the other partner should provide reassurance to help manage that feeling. For instance, sometimes the betrayed believes that the best way they can manage their feelings of insecurity is by the constant surveillance of the unfaithful or by blocking the unfaithful's access to temptation via limiting interactions with others. This may seem like a good way to provide reassurance to the betrayed at first glance, but, when you look closer, you will realize that it's a fake sense of security because those measures don't really get at the core of the issue. Also, it only guarantees that the unfaithful is behaving well when they are being watched.

The Challenge of the Bipolar Nature of Healing

As stated before, in order for couples to heal from the trauma of infidelity, they have to process a lot of uncomfortable feelings and thoughts with one another. In order for this sharing to take place, it requires the partners to be vulnerable. This usually puts them in two binds—one: surviving the emotional swings without losing track of progress; and two: maintaining intimacy without interfering with the healing process.

Healing from infidelity is not a linear process. If we try to put the progress of healing on a graph, we will not see a steady incline in improvement. Instead, we will see a jagged line with peaks and valleys that eventually even out to a steady incline. The peaks and valleys are caused by the emotional swings that happen as a result of the higher level of sharing and processing of feelings and thoughts with one another.

This level of sharing builds intimacy because both partners are willing to be open with one another with their raw thoughts and feelings. This naturally makes couples feel drawn closer together, but, paradoxically, this level of sharing will also cause a lot of pain and discomfort for both partners.

Couples experience intense desires to be emotionally and physically intimate with one another accompanied with feelings of guilt, shame, hurt, and anger occurring as a result of the content of what was shared. The challenge faced by couples here is to refrain from seeing the desire to be intimate with one another as a sign of weakness. This is difficult to accomplish because couples usually worry that the desire to be intimate might imply that all is forgiven and the healing work is done. What I tell all my clients is that there is nothing wrong with having the conflicting feelings for intimacy, anger, hurt, and shame as long as the two of you are able to keep those feelings in context. In other words, don't overestimate their worth, meaning, don't take them as a sign that all is forgiven but, also, don't minimize their impact by assuming that they are just fleeting or insignificant. It's best to accept them as natural feelings in the moment they are being experienced.

The Challenge of Living a Normal Life During Abnormal Times

Life doesn't stop just because you are dealing with an affair. It would be nice if we all had the luxury to take time off from our duties and responsibilities to heal from infidelity, but, unfortunately, that is not usually an option. This fact is one of the main reasons why a lot of couples fail in recovering from affairs, simply because they don't have the time to deal with it properly, especially when considering that they still have to go to work, pay the bills, raise the kids, etc.

This issue becomes more complicated when considering that you still have to hide the details of what is going on between you and your partner from family, friends, and the outside world. The challenge here is finding the time and energy needed to heal while trying to maintain a sense of normalcy that is needed to continue to follow through with your duties and responsibilities.

Many couples struggle with finding the right balance which leads them to feel helpless. This is why it's important to utilize as much help and support as possible from people that are close to you during this difficult time. This is the time in which I encourage couples to find a way to temporarily modify their work situation to allow for time and space needed to deal with the affair. If you are able to take some time off, do so. If you are able to reduce hours or flex schedules, do so as well. Sometimes, you will need alone time with your partner to talk things out or attend counseling sessions. Other times, you might just need alone time to help you process and cope. These are the times where you ask family and friends to help you babysit or take the kids to games and extracurricular activities. Your boss, family, and friends don't need to know the specifics of your situation. All they need to know is that you are dealing with a family or relationship crisis that needs your immediate attention. People will understand and respect your boundaries.

Another issue couples face in regard to the need to continue normalcy is the fear of sending the wrong message to one another about where they stand in terms of the healing process. Couples worry that acting normal for the sake of survival or possibly for the sake of the kids, who should not be privy to the knowledge of the affair, might cause confusion by making one or both partners think all is well and all is forgiven. There is also the fact that acting normal will bring up feelings of anger, sadness, and resentment because this will remind the couple of how the affair has tainted this normalcy. My advice to my clients is to accept these feelings as a normal part of the healing process and continue to remind themselves that acting normal can be just what it is, acting, and does not mean that all is forgiven and fixed. It's merely a tool that needs to be used to help us follow through with our responsibilities while we are working on healing.

Step 4: Seeking Professional Help

There are a lot of issues and topics individuals and couples can fix on their own through self-help books. Healing from infidelity is not one of those issues. "Then why did I buy this book?" you might ask. This book was written to serve as a map for you and your partner to help you navigate your way from despair to healing. It's one of the best maps that you can find that describes the roads to that destination and all the perils you will face and overcome to get there safely. But, at the end of the day, even the best map is useless if you don't have an experienced guide that can help you navigate through the difficulties. This is the same reason mountain climbers need Sherpas.

There are three different venues that I recommend to my clients when it comes to seeking professional help: couples counseling, individual counseling, and support groups. People who have the most success are the ones who can go with the triple threat, incorporating all three venues for their support. Some can only afford to go with one venue. In those scenarios, I highly recommend that you go with couples counseling. Below, you will find a description of the qualities that you should be looking for in each venue.

Couples Counseling

The thing that most people don't know is that not all therapists are well-trained and experienced in working with couples. Most therapists receive generalized training which allows them to work with individuals, couples, and families. But only few are trained and experienced in working with couples, and even fewer are trained and specialized in helping couples dealing with infidelity.

The first thing you should look for is a professional who is licensed to do counseling. Each state has different classifications and types of licensure required to conduct counseling, but the general ones are Licensed Marriage and Family Therapist, Licensed Social Worker, and Licensed Psychologist. The second thing to look for is specialties and types of training received that gives the counselor the expertise needed to perform that specialty. The third thing to look for is their track record, i.e.: years of experience, number of clients worked with, and success rate. Lastly, and most importantly, you need to look for compatibility of personalities and counseling approach.

This one gets a little bit tricky because there are many different variables that can play a part, but not all are pertinent. My recommendation is to find a counselor who has a solution focused approach to counseling, i.e. not only someone who helps you by listening and allowing you the space to process your thoughts and feelings, but someone who also gives you the tools and skills needed to fix the problem. You want a counselor who is not afraid to hold you and your partner accountable for the part you played as well as the agreement you come up with. You also need a counselor who is able to maintain neutrality and is able to help you see both sides of the issue. I tell my clients, "My job is to be a mirror and not an echo. I will reflect to you what I see and tell you what needs to happen to fix it, but I will not repeat to you what you want to hear."

You also want a counselor who is interested in helping you get unstuck in the direction that is best suited for you and your partner's needs. You need someone who will not let their personal bias interfere with the reality of your situation and your needs and abilities as a couple to heal together or separately.

Individual Counseling

The purpose of individual counseling is to help provide each of you the support you need to get through this difficult process. It's hard for the betrayed to empathize with the unfaithful and help them through their struggles. It's also difficult for the betrayed to vent to the unfaithful and rely on them for emotional support because they happen to be the cause of their pain. So, in a nutshell, individual counseling will give both of you the individual space to vent and process your own feelings and thoughts during this difficult time. Keep in mind that this is not a space for secrets and talking trash; it's simply a space in which the full attention is being dedicated to the individual versus the couple.

It's ideal if the individual sessions are provided by the same counselor who is also providing the couples counseling. The benefit of this is twofold—one: he or she is already aware of the couple's dynamics which means there should be no concerns about misrepresentation or half-truths; and two: when couples use the same counselor for both individual and couples sessions, the counselor is able to utilize what is gained in the individual sessions to enhance the progress in the couples sessions. Some couples prefer to see different counselors for the individual sessions, which is okay to do as long as you are able to find a counselor who is willing and able to communicate about the progress with the couple's counselor and also proceed toward the same goals and directions being sought after in the couples sessions. In other words, you want to avoid having two guides who are going in different directions.

Support Groups

Support groups for couples and individuals who are dealing with infidelity are rare, but they do exist. The benefit of attending a support group is knowing that you are not alone in this and also getting to learn more about your experience through the experiences of others. What you want to look for in a support group is peers who are in the same situation as you, to a certain extent, i.e. unfaithfuls attend unfaithfuls' groups and betrayed attend betrayed groups. You also need to be aware of the agenda of the group facilitator and their particular view on infidelity and how to deal with it. There are a lot of support groups that are hosted by churches who have their own spiritual views about marriage and infidelity, as well as specific directions and agendas for guiding members toward a particular outcome. You also want to make sure that whatever support group you attend is a group that is well facilitated, i.e. it's conducted with the guidance of a licensed professional or a very experienced peer— someone who is keeping an eye on misinformation and poor, unhealthy group dynamics.

Setting up the stage for healing is not an easy task, but it's an important one because it impacts your ability to complete the next milestones in the healing process. This is why it's important to take the necessary time and utilize the appropriate resources to set the stage properly. This is not the time to rush or cut corners. It's the time fort thoughtful consideration followed by a firm commitment to invest in your future wellbeing.

Chapter 5

The Second Milestone:
Getting the Story

"For every good reason there is to lie, there is a
better reason to tell the truth."

---Bo Bennett

Now that you've set the stage for healing, it's time to roll up your sleeves and take on the first important step of getting the story of what happened. Some of you might have taken this step already. For others, that step has not taken place yet. It's my job to provide you with all the information that you need to assure that this step was done correctly. Failing to do so will impact the whole healing process. So, whether or not you believe you've completed this step already, keep reading to make sure that you didn't miss any crucial aspects.

Why Is It Important to Get the Story?

One of the main ways humans process information is through the power of narrative. Stories are some of the tools we use to help us make sense of the world around us and the experiences we have. The reason that stories are able to help in that way is because they allow us to organize a large number of various pieces of information about an event in a cohesive framework.

This framework makes it easier to figure out why things happened, understand cause and effect, and draw conclusions about how bad a situation is. All of these benefits help us form opinions we act upon once we have managed to make sense of what happened. This is a long way to say that the actions people take are based on the stories they have about what took place.

In regard to infidelity, getting the story will give you and your partner an opportunity to understand what happened and why it happened, which will help you decide on the best steps to take to deal with it. This is why it behooves the two of you to be able to tell and hear the true story of what took place, instead of a twisted version of it. Twisted stories beget twisted actions; true stories beget true actions. Catch my drift?

The Trifecta of Truth

Telling the truth about what happened and being able to listen to it and accept it without twisting the facts is a challenging process. It's challenging because our emotions at times get in the way of telling the truth as well as hearing it. Some emotions like guilt, fear, and shame force us to filter the truth to make it less ugly. Other emotions like anger, hurt, and sadness work as blinders that only allow us to accept the version of the truth that sustains the existence of theses emotions. So, how do we expect to get to the truth without shutting down our emotions? In order to do that, you need to have three elements: proactive transparency, suspension of disbelief, and controlled content.

One: Proactive Transparency

Transparency is like living in a glass house in which there are no barriers or covers to obscure what's contained within. Everything is out there in the open for everyone to see, if they wish to do so. The wish to do so part is what makes it more of a passive stance i.e., "Everything is there, if you want to see it; I am not going to stop you, but I also won't go out of my way to show you certain things that you may not like."

Transparency is important because it achieves the goal of keeping everything in the open which helps in building trust. But, because of its passivity, it fails to take that goal a step further. This is why I ask my clients to adopt the stance of proactive transparency. This is a stance in which simply keeping everything in the open isn't enough. One must also take additional efforts to highlight and showcase things that should be brought to awareness without waiting for someone to probe or ask. Proactive transparency builds trust and displays a willingness and readiness for accountability.

What Are the Barriers for Proactive Transparency?

The benefits of proactive transparency are not free and sometimes the sticker price itself can be the barrier that prevents couples from taking such a stance. In order for a couple to be proactively transparent, they have to take two risks: the risk of exposure and the risk of impact.

The risk of exposure takes place when we lift the veil and allow our partner to see everything—the good, the bad, and anything in between. This means that we are leaving ourselves vulnerable and trusting that our vulnerability will not be misused or abused. This usually prevents couples from being proactively transparent because they worry that whatever they reveal is going to be used against them for purposes other than that of healing, such as divorce proceedings, custody battles, revenge, punishment, humiliation, and so on.

The risk of impact takes place because we don't really have any control over how what's being revealed is going to impact the person who is now privy to what was hidden before. That person is not just your partner. Sometimes that person is you, because, believe it or not, sometimes we are not transparent with ourselves. The content of what will be revealed will not only affect how you and your partner will feel about yourselves and each other, but it will also impact what actions you are going to take as a result of those feelings. To put things into perspective, not all of your feelings are going to be valid, and, therefore, not all the actions are going to be healthy and conducive to conflict resolution. What prevents couples from being proactive here is the desire to prevent further pain and harm to the betrayed, the need to avoid seeing oneself in a negative light, and the fear that telling the truth will change the decision about fixing the relationship.

How to Create a Safe Environment for Proactive Transparency

It doesn't matter how much we highlight the benefits of proactive transparency and how sold you are on the concept and its necessity to heal you. What matters is helping you create the right environment that makes you and your partner feel safe to take such a risky stance. For that to happen, you and your partner will need to make three agreements about the scope of use, feeling exploration and management, and accepting outcomes.

Scope of Use Agreement

There are good reasons and bad reasons for wanting proactive transparency. Good reasons are ones that fall under the category of using what's revealed to understand what took place in order to heal solo or together. Bad reasons are anything that stems from the motivation to punish or get even. Think constructive use versus destructive use.

Obviously, we want to use the revealed information in a constructive way. This means that the two of you have to agree on a definition of what constructive use means, and you must be crystal clear about the expectations that correlate with your understanding of that definition.

The best rule for determining how the information should be used is by focusing on what happened, why it happened, and where to go from there. Meaning, we are not using the information to fight each other in court or go after the third party for revenge and retribution, or using it to humiliate and punish one another because we are in pain.

Feelings Exploration and Management Agreement

This is the same point that I highlight and emphasize throughout the entire book, which is to be prepared, ready, and willing to experience many uncomfortable feelings during this whole process. You and your partner have to agree to refrain from sugar-coating the truth just because you want to avoid looking and feeling bad or because you don't want to cause further pain to your partner.

Affairs are painful events by their nature. It's like being shot with an explosive bullet that leaves shrapnel in your body. In order to survive and prevent further damage, you have to perform the painful act of removing those sharp pieces. So yes, being transparent and telling the truth will hurt you and your partner because both of you will have to admit to and hear things that you didn't want to accept, hear or believe about yourself, your relationship, and each other. But, avoiding this pain will only make things worse, because a proper healing cannot take place without removing the shrapnel. Bottom line, the two of you have to accept that pain to self and one another is a necessary evil for getting better.

Accepting the need to face and experience those negative feelings is one of the important steps in the right direction. What needs to follow is the effective processing and management of these feelings in a way that is conducive to healing. The best way to effectively manage all kinds of negative feelings is to correctly answer three basic questions. Those questions are: what am I feeling? Is that feeling appropriate to the situation? And what is the best way to let this feeling run its course in a way that will achieve the most desired outcome?

For example, often times the unfaithful tries to avoid being transparent about the truth of what took place to avoid feeling "bad." But feeling "bad" is a very general label to a feeling that doesn't really give us any valuable data that we can use to understand what's going on in our life.

This is why the unfaithful has to ask the first question, "What am I feeling?" In this example, if the unfaithful takes some time to zoom in on the specific feelings, he or she will most likely realize that the feeling they are experiencing is shame. Shame is a very uncomfortable feeling to experience for everyone regardless of circumstances. Now, let's move on to question number two, "Is this feeling appropriate to the situation?" Well, yes, because shame is a legitimate and valid feeling to have when someone does something wrong, especially when they were fully aware of the wrongness of that action. Third question, "What is the best way to let this feeling run its course in a way that will achieve the most desired outcome?" The best way here is for the unfaithful to acknowledge they did something wrong, apologize for the wrong doing, figure out why he or she did it, and come up with a plan to prevent it from happening ever again.

Accepting Outcomes Agreement

As I mentioned early on, most couples wish to have an outcome in which both can stay together and fix the relationship. But, the reality of the situation is that not everyone can have that ending. Sometimes ending the relationship is the right and healthy option, especially if the couple finds out that one or both don't have what it takes to make this relationship work in a way that satisfies the needs of everyone involved.

A lot of couples struggle with this view because we are all trained to accept the idea that love is all you need to fix everything. This notion is a myth. Don't get me wrong. Love is a necessary ingredient that is needed to sustain a healthy relationship, but, if it's not backed up by actions, it becomes a useless feeling in the heart.

In order for the couple to heal, they have to take action. They can't take action if they don't understand what happed and why it happened. In order to achieve that understanding they need to know the true story. If they don't have the true story, then their actions are going to be misguided. What I tell my clients is, if you are interested in real solutions, then you have to be honest with yourself and each other about the story of the affair.

Dishonesty will only lead to future problems. In other words, telling the truth gives you a chance to save your relationship, especially if you and your partner have what it takes to fix it. But twisting the truth is a guarantee that your relationship will fail, maybe not right away, but eventually it will catch up to you, and it won't be pretty. The take home message is that you and your partner have to make a commitment to exploring the truth regardless of what outcome it will lead to.

Two: Suspension of Disbelief

Once you and your partner create a safe environment for proactive transparency, you have to overcome the challenge of disbelief. The reason disbelief exists in the first place is because infidelity usually involves a great level of deception. This makes it difficult for the betrayed to believe the unfaithful is telling them the truth about what happened. How do you know that a liar is telling you the truth now? I call this, the-boy-who-cried-wolf dilemma. You know that he lied a great deal of times, but you also know that he is capable of telling the truth. The tricky part is learning how to tell the difference.

The reason it's difficult for the betrayed to believe the story of the unfaithful is because they are looking for tangible evidence to support the story. The only problem here is that no such proof exists. It's true that people can hire a private detective to take pictures and track visits. People can also dig up phone records and social media accounts. But none of these things reveal the full truth of what took place. Because, the only two people who know the full truth about the affair are the unfaithful and the third party.

However, just because we don't have tangible evidence capturing every physical and emotional moment of the affair, does not mean we can't find the truth. This just means that we have to use a different approach to seeking it other than tangible evidence that does not exist. Because, if that was the only way for people to discover the truth, no one would ever get convicted or cleared in a court of law.

So how can the betrayed suspend his or her disbelief? Well, what I encourage the betrayed to do is use logic to deduce whether or not the unfaithful is telling the truth. The process of this deduction will utilize reason to see if the story details fall in line with common sense, partner's personality, and whatever known and substantiated facts there are about the details of the affair. This is a process that is best achieved if facilitated by a couples counselor with a good nose for BS. Another thing that helps the suspension of disbelief is to make sure that the safe environment for truth was created, and that all the secondary motives were ruled out. If these elements were clearly proven during the counseling sessions, then logic dictates that it would be foolish for the unfaithful to continue to tell lies, especially when considering that it would be counterproductive to achieving what they want, which is fixing the relationship.

Three: Content Control

At this point, you already understand the value of telling the story and the tools needed to tell it truthfully. Now we need to talk about what's appropriate, healthy, and helpful to know and what is not. This determination can't be made solely by the betrayed or the unfaithful, because each has their own motivation and feelings that influences their view on what is appropriate to share and know.

In my counseling sessions, I guide the process of telling the story by refereeing the questions asked and the answers provided. I do it because some couples either ask too little or too much, both of which can cause a different kind of harm to the process. Too little won't tell us anything about the cause of the affair, and too much will give the couple unnecessary details that can linger long after the affair.

My job is to help the betrayed figure out what questions to ask, understand why they are asking the questions, and determine the value that will be gained by getting the answers to those questions. My job with the unfaithful is to make sure they are providing truthful, satisfactory answers that address the need underlying the questions. The point here is that both the unfaithful and the betrayed need to understand what they are asking, why are they asking it, and what they will gain from the answer.

For example, it's legitimate for the betrayed to ask the unfaithful about the frequency and types of interaction he or she had with the third party, but they don't need to know the nitty gritty details of each interaction, because none of those details are going to serve a useful purpose other than providing unpleasant imagery in the betrayed's head.

Once again, I highly recommend that the milestone of getting the story takes place under the guidance of an experienced infidelity specialist to assure that it's conducted in the best way to achieve success. If you are planning to do it on your own, then make sure that your questions have a useful purpose, such as, how long has the affair been going on, what caused it, and can it be fixed? Also make sure that you are keeping this between you two. In other words, don't try to get any details or confirmations from outside sources, such as the third party or their partner if the third party was also in a committed relationship. Any information you receive from outside sources will be influenced by the other source's motivations. Those motivations compromise the integrity of the data received and can cause more harm than good.

Things to Keep in Mind

Asking questions and providing answers are some of the main ways that will help the couple get the true story. But, you also have to be open to other ways that can help in this process. The rule of thumb here is that those ways need to be healthy, reliable, and judged within their own context. So, if the betrayed asked for access to phone, emails, social media history, etc., there shouldn't be any resistance from the unfaithful as long as the need for that access has a healthy, constructive purpose that is aimed at getting the truth versus unnecessary details.

Getting the story is not a milestone that you can check off your list and never need to revisit, but it also can't be something that goes on for the rest of your natural life. There is no magic number of times of how often the story needs to be retold and questioned. This is based on the fact that each person processes things differently and each relationship has its own unique set of factors. To me, the need for telling the truth and questioning the story will end when two things happen—one: the questions asked were answered in a satisfactory way; and two: the betrayed made a conscious choice to accept the story and move forward to the next step of healing.

This is why it's crucial for the couple to commit to moving forward when this milestone is completed. Meaning, the betrayed must make a commitment to stop revisiting texts, emails, phone records, or anything related to retelling the story, once both agree that the story was told to everyone's satisfaction. Sometimes the betrayed feels the need to hang on to evidence of the affair or continue to dig up or question certain pieces of information past the point of satisfaction. Such efforts will only prolong the healing process and prevent both partners from moving forward. At such a point, those efforts will no longer be a normal process of trying to get the story but instead become an obsession that ties the couple to a very strong chain.

This means that it's in the couple's best interest to be as thoughtful and diligent as they can possibly be to make sure that getting the story milestone is completed successfully. This will allow the two of you to move on to the next steps in the healing process without having to dwell in the past.

Chapter 6

The Third Milestone:
Acknowledging the Impact

"Taking responsibility for being exactly where you are gives you the power to be exactly where you want to be."

---Author Unknown

Now that you and your partner have managed to get the story of the affair, it's time to take the next step of acknowledging the impact of that story on your lives. Infidelity leaves a huge impact on the lives of the people who are involved in the affair. Not only does it impact the unfaithful, the betrayed, and the third party, but it also impacts their friends and family members. Needless to say, such an impact is never positive and often causes significant emotional damage. When we get hurt emotionally, we usually respond in one of two ways: shutting down or lashing out, neither of which is conducive to mending relationships.

This means that the impact of infidelity is an enormous negative force that has the potential for causing irreversible damage to the relationship. In order for us to mitigate its effects and recover from its damage, we have to truly understand it. This is why this milestone is important to the healing process. Skipping this step or handling it poorly will most likely lead to relationship ruin.

In order for us to begin to understand anything, first we have to acknowledge its existence. This is also true in the case of the impact of infidelity. If you want to understand it to mitigate its effects, you and your partner have to acknowledge its existence. Acknowledging the impact of infidelity is a three-pronged process that encompasses thoughts, feelings, and actions. It's the ability to articulate your understanding of the damage caused, followed by your ability to express the appropriate feelings related to that understanding, and your ability to act on those feelings in appropriate ways that are conducive to mending the relationship.

The three-pronged process is necessary because doing it any other way will be incomplete. For example, if couples only focus on the intellectual aspect, you will get statements like, "I understand that cheating on you caused you to feel hurt." This statement alone doesn't demonstrate to me anything other than the unfaithful has the capacity to understand cause and effect. This is nice to know but not very useful as a standalone item, especially if it's not accompanied with any kind of emotions that the unfaithful should experience and express as a result of that intellectual understanding.

So, what happens when couples only focus on the emotional aspect of acknowledgment? Well you get statement like, "I feel bad that you are feeling hurt." The only thing that this statement demonstrates is that the unfaithful has the capacity for empathy, which once again is a nice thing to know, but useless if it's not accompanied by the unfaithful's understanding that his or her actions are the cause of that hurt and pain.

Sometimes couples ignore the expression of the intellectual understating of cause and effect, and the expression of the appropriate emotions that should accompany that understanding and jump right into actions that they believe will fix the problem, like buying flowers or stepping up their game when it comes to doing what is expected of them as partners.

Even though these are positive actions, they are considered phony if they are not motivated by genuine thoughts and feelings. There is no point in taking thoughtless actions that are not motivated by authentic emotions. Phony actions are not sustainable because they lack substance.

The Benefits of Acknowledging the Impact of Infidelity

Validation and Empathy

Infidelity impacts couples because it produces painful emotions like anger, betrayal, mistrust, guilt, and shame. Those emotions are not easy to feel or be subjected to. But, in order for the couple to move forward, they have to manage those emotions effectively in ways that would allow for the best possible outcome.

In order to manage these emotions, validation has to take place. Meaning, we have to accept why those emotions are being experienced despite our discomfort with their existence. Validation can't take place without acknowledging impact. In other words, in order for the unfaithful to accept the betrayed's feelings of anger, betrayal, and pain, they must have the ability to acknowledge that their actions are what caused the existence of those emotions. Refusing to make that acknowledgement will only lead to the escalation of those emotions, which almost always leads to poor conflict resolution.

***

Accountability

The process of acknowledging the impact of infidelity has a built-in accountability tool. One of the key components of acknowledgment is the articulation of the understanding of cause and effect. Such an acknowledgement cannot take place without highlighting who was responsible for the act that caused the effect.

Accountability allows you to take responsibility for your actions. Taking responsibility for your actions allows you to experience the appropriate emotions related to the effect of your actions. People who are able to be accountable for their actions have access to a moral compass that guides their future decisions. The idea here is simple; if you have the ability to comprehend how much damage your actions have caused others, you will feel bad about what you did. The bad feelings should be a deterrent for making similar poor decisions in the future. So, knowing that both the unfaithful and the betrayed have the ability to be accountable for their actions provides hope and reassurance in each other's ability to avoid being in the same situation in the future.

Damage Assessment

The impact of infidelity changes how couples function and interact with one another. Sometimes it's difficult for couples to see the changes in their functioning within its contexts without making misassumptions about the change's source.

The process of acknowledging the impact of infidelity requires a thorough understanding of the gravity of the mistakes made as well as the damage those mistakes caused. This process of assessment allows the couple to determine how much and what kind of damage was caused by the affair versus other factors related to preexisting issues prior to the affair. The assessment of the damage will help the couple ascertain whether or not the relationship is salvageable. This, in return, will help the couple identify the appropriate steps to take toward fixing the damage.

***

The Impact of Infidelity

As mentioned earlier, the impact of infidelity is not only limited to the betrayed. The negative consequences of affairs affect everyone whose lives are connected to the unfaithful, the betrayed, and the third party. Infidelity can have clear, tangible, physical impacts like contracting and sharing sexually transmitted diseases, unwanted pregnancies, and job losses because of affairs in the workplace. Infidelity can also have less tangible emotional impacts that affect both partners differently. The impacts manifest through intense, painful emotions. Those emotions often lead to impulsive actions. Those actions consequently change the dynamics of the relationship between the couple. Each person experiences the impact of infidelity differently, even the ones who are experiencing it from the same vantage point of the role they played in the affair. So, here is a description of the impact of some of the common emotions experienced by the couples I have worked with throughout the years:

Impact of Anger

The Betrayed's Perspective

The betrayed feels enraged because they were wronged by the actions of the unfaithful. We all feel angry whenever we are disrespected and betrayed. Disrespect is born when boundaries are breached and when lines get crossed. Betrayal is born when we get tricked or mislead by those we love for the sake of fulfilling their needs at the expense of ours. For the most part, the betrayed's anger stems from the general sense of unfairness of the whole situation. Other times, the betrayed are angry with themselves for "allowing this to happen," or "not seeing the writing on the wall."

The anger toward the unfaithful can manifest through impulsive words and actions geared toward reciprocating that same disrespect and betrayal, and attempts to even out the scale. This can range from verbal and physical assaults to committing similar acts of infidelity. Feeling betrayed destroys the loyalty that partners are supposed to have for one another. This usually compels the betrayed to start acting only on what's in their best interest, especially when considering the fact that this is exactly what their partner has done. The anger toward self usually takes the form of self-loathing and blaming oneself for the affair. Sometimes this can lead to making excuses for the unfaithful instead of holding them accountable for their part.

The Unfaithful's Perspective

The unfaithful usually feel angry because they were found out and can no longer continue living the lie they created. We usually get angry when we are prevented from doing things we want to do, regardless of how good or bad these things are for us. This is called frustration. The unfaithful also feel angry with themselves when they realize the destructive consequences of their poor choices. A lot of unfaithful report feeling disgusted with themselves for committing such acts.

The anger can manifest through the expression of frustration. This takes place because the unfaithful feel they are being asked to give up the only outlet they have to fulfill their unmet needs without providing them with another viable alternative for those needs. The anger toward self usually takes the form of self-deprecation accompanied with a sense of worthlessness which usually leads to shutting down.

Impact of Sadness

The Betrayed's Perspective

The betrayed feels sad because they are hurting. The unfaithful broke their heart, let them down, and now they feel lost. The heart broke when trust was abused. Nothing can break a heart better than being stabbed in the back by your best friend. The letdown comes from the fact that the unfaithful did not live up to the expectation of exclusivity and what the betrayed thought to be true about them and their character. Feeling lost is the result of the betrayed's world turning upside down and the betrayed finding out that what they thought they knew about their partner and their relationship is no longer true.

Feeling hurt often compels the betrayed to want to hurt the unfaithful back. Other times, the betrayed deals with the hurt by withdrawing, trying to bury the pain, and building a wall around their heart to prevent future hurt. This takes the form of emotional disconnection and avoidance of vulnerability.

The Unfaithful's Perspective

The unfaithful feel sad because they become aware of their partner's pain as a result of their actions which causes them to feel pain as well. The unfaithful also feel sad because they have also let themselves down by choosing poor ways to fulfill their needs. This feeling of disappointment in oneself also leads to feeling lost, because the unfaithful realize that they are not living up to their moral code.

Another source of sadness will come as a result of grieving the loss of the relationship the unfaithful had with the third party. This is usually experienced in the emotional type of affairs, in which the unfaithful developed a strong emotional bond. Ending the affair is often experienced in the same fashion as a break up.

The overall impact of all of this sadness can compel the unfaithful to withdraw to avoid causing more harm to the betrayed. Other times, the unfaithful try to escape that feeling through substance abuse and other unhealthy behaviors.

Impact of Fear

The Betrayed's Perspective

One of the major ways that fear impacts the betrayed is through insecurity. The source of insecurity comes from the inescapable fact that the unfaithful went to someone else to fulfill his or her needs instead of going to his/her partner. Regardless of the specific factors that led to the affair, it's difficult for the betrayed to avoid comparing themselves to the third party. That comparison is the root of insecurity. Because, the common thought on the betrayed's mind is, "They must have liked the other person more than they liked me; why else would they stray?"

That feeling of insecurity destroys the betrayed's self-esteem. Low self-esteem leads to many different trajectories in behavior, none of which are positive. Some people try to overcompensate by promiscuity and reckless behaviors, while others isolate, shut down, and abuse substances.

Another way that fear impacts the betrayed is through worries. Worries are fears that are related to things that are unknown. The scope of the type of worries is vast and extends to the past and the future. A common worry about the past is whether or not the whole relationship was a sham and the implication of that realization, if it was determined to be true. A common worry about the future is, "How is this going to impact our family, or what if I make the wrong choice?"

Worries can cause the betrayed to act in ways that make them hesitant, indecisive, and doubtful. This leads to tremendous amounts of stress and frustration caused by the failure to act and make choices during a time that requires taking action.

The Unfaithful's Perspective

The impact of fear on the unfaithful is heavily weighted on future outcomes. One source of this fear stems from the shock factor when confronted with their own ability to act selfishly with plain disregard to consequences. The other source comes from the uncertainty about the betrayed's ability to forgive and rebuild trust.

The shock can cause the unfaithful to begin questioning all the different aspects of their life that they never had to question before. Think of it as casting a big cloud of doubt over what used to be a sun-shiny spot of clarity. This doubt also leads to hesitation and indecisiveness, which can impede the ability to take necessary action to heal and move forward.

The uncertainty about the betrayed's ability to forgive and move past the trauma can lead to a sense of hopelessness about the future. This usually translates to apathy and a lack of action: "He/She is never going to be able to forgive me and move past this, so why even bother?'

***

The Impact of Shame

The Betrayed's Perspective

A lot of people are surprised to hear that the betrayed often experiences shame, even though they are the victim of the act of infidelity. We usually feel ashamed whenever we are dishonored. The unfaithful dishonor their partners when they decide to have an affair, because they tarnish the sanctity of the relationship contract.

Dishonoring someone makes them feel worthless, and, when you feel worthless, you become apathetic and withdrawn because nothing really matters. This apathy gets in the way of taking the actions needed to heal and move forward.

The Unfaithful's Perspective

The unfaithful are the ones who are most impacted by shame. This has to do with the fact that their actions are what lead to the situation that they are currently in. The cause of this shame comes from guilt and defamation.

The unfaithful feel defamed because their partners have caught them doing something that is universally agreed upon as a horrible thing to do to another human being. Now they feel embarrassed that their partners have seen their shortcoming and possibly have shared this with others who will no longer see them how they used to be seen prior to the knowledge of the affair. So, what do people do when they are embarrassed? They run away and hide or act out in anger, neither of which is helpful to processing the trauma of the affair or conducive to resolving conflict.

As for the feeling of guilt, it's simply the natural consequence of doing something bad that causes others to suffer. Guilt can be a positive force that can be used as a deterrent for future indiscretion. But it can also be a negative force if the unfaithful allows it to interfere with the healing process. Guilt is a very unpleasant thing to experience, so, often times, the unfaithful try to take unhealthy shortcuts to speed up the healing process to avoid feeling guilty or they minimize the length of that experience.

This is usually done through avoidance or distractions. Avoidance takes the form of refusing to discuss details or talk about the affair. Distractions take the form of shifting the focus away from self by addressing seemingly relevant issues. Other forms of distraction are overcompensating acts like buying gifts, honeymoon trips, etc., that are motivated to put a band-aid on the problem rather than solving it.

Concrete Steps to Acknowledge the Impact of Infidelity

Now that we have covered the significance of this process as well as the different components it contains, it's time to walk you through the right steps to complete it successfully. Keep in mind that even though acknowledging the impact of infidelity is going to be done primarily by the unfaithful, the betrayed will also have to acknowledge how the unfaithful are being impacted by infidelity. It's important to emphasize that this is not a script you should mimic like a parrot. It's a guideline on what points you need to hit. Say it in your own words, and be genuine.

Step 1: Articulate your understanding of how your actions led to the emotional consequences experienced by your partner, and take ownership of that understanding.

"I understand that my infidelity caused you to feel _____, and I take full responsibility and ownership of my actions and the consequences they have caused."

Be very specific about highlighting the correct emotions that you believe your partner is experiencing. Don't just give broad terms like sad. You need to think of what kind of sad and at what intensity, such as, "heartbroken." Also, be open to the possibility that your perception of what you think your partner is experiencing emotionally may be incomplete or inaccurate. So, make it a point to ask them whether or not the feeling you have identified is accurate and whether or not there were other feelings you missed.

***

Step 2: Validate your partner's emotional experience.

"I can truly see why my infidelity has caused you to have these feelings."

It's very important here to go beyond conveying that you understand why your actions produced those feelings. You also must emphasize to your partner that you believe that these are the only valid and logical feelings to have as a reaction toward such actions. It's like the difference between saying, *"I can see why you might feel that way,"* versus *"You have every right to feel that way."*

Step 3: Articulate your understanding of how these feelings are impacting your partner's behavior and functioning.

"I understand that feeling heartbroken makes you want to disconnect emotionally and build a wall around your heart."

This step is tricky because it seems like you are encouraging your partner to deal with the emotions they are feeling in a way that is not healthy or conducive to healing. This is why you need to remember that what you are saying in this step is that you simply understand why your partner is behaving in such a way. Expressing that understanding will allow your partner the opportunity to reexamine better ways to deal with these feelings.

Step 4: Provide a sincere apology.

"I am very sorry that I broke your heart with my infidelity, and, because of that, you now feel that you have to be emotionally withdrawn to protect your heart."

The key to doing this step correctly is to make it strictly centered on the apology, no more, no less. This is not the place for providing explanations for what you did and why you did it. The apology needs to be heartfelt and in line with the gravity of the damage for which you are apologizing.

Step 5: Express how you feel about realizing the impact of your actions on your partner.

"I feel very guilty for breaking your heart."

Once again, pin-pointing the exact emotion and the intensity that is being experienced is key. In addition to identifying the exact emotion, you need to identify the intensity of that emotion. Simply identifying and stating what you feel is one part of this process. The other part is to show that feeling. In other words, if you are feeling sad, I need to see that instead of just taking your word for it. Show me what sad looks like on the outside. Don't be afraid have those feelings manifest as long as they are done appropriately.

Step 6: Articulate how the feelings you are experiencing as a result of acknowledging the impact of your actions are influencing your behavior and functioning.

"My feelings of guilt are what compels me to avoid discussing the details of the affair or make attempts to distract attention away from it."

There are two things to avoid during this step: blaming your partner for how you feel and justifying the unhealthy actions associated with those feelings. The best way to do that is by emphasizing your understanding of your responsibility for those feelings and by making a commitment for choosing healthy behaviors and actions to deal with these feelings.

Step 7: Ask your partner what they need from you to help them process their emotions and act on them in ways that are conducive to healing.

"What can I do and how can I help you with the emotional damage I have caused?"

Be prepared for the fact that your partner may not have a clear answer or may not be ready to provide one. That doesn't mean you are off the hook because you can still ask them what you can do to help them get to that answer. You have to be respectful for the time and space they need to get to that point. You also have to trust in their ability to know their own needs. In other words, what they might ask of you may not seem very helpful if you were in their shoes. This is why you have to remind yourself that they are not you, and you have to provide them with what's going to work for them as long as what they are asking for is healthy and conducive to healing.

Step 8: Ask your partner about their expectations of you in regard to dealing with your own emotions.

"I know that distraction and avoidance are not good ways for me to deal with my guilt; how are you expecting me to act on those feelings?"

This step allows you and your partner to have an open discussion about the best ways for you two to deal with these difficult and intense emotions in ways that will help bring you closer together instead of driving you apart. Think of it as a collaborative step in which you help each other figure out the best way to behave during this difficult time, despite the pull toward unhealthy behaviors. It's important that whatever expectations the two of you agree on are ones that are relevant to the issue at hand and are going to produce a positive outcome. This means that the two of you have to monitor the effectiveness of living up to those expectations and whether or not they are making things better or worse so that you can readjust accordingly.

Challenges and Pitfalls

To ensure that you have the best chances for success in completing this milestone, you have to be aware of and prepared for some of the challenges and pitfalls that you will encounter. Having that awareness is helpful because it normalizes your experience and gives you a chance to come up with a plan of action to face those challenges. Here are some of the common challenges faced by my clients:

Different Vantage Point

In order for couples to acknowledge the impact of infidelity, they have to access, explore, express, and share their emotional experiences. The type and intensity of emotions as well as the time it will take to process them successfully will vary drastically between the unfaithful and the betrayed.

The reason behind this vast difference is the fact that both played a different role which translates to different actions, reactions, consequences, and feelings related to those actions and consequences. Furthermore, the unfaithful has had a head start on the emotional experience simply because he or she was aware of the affair way before the betrayed got wind of it.

The main effect of that head start can be seen in intensity of these emotions experienced by both partners and the time expected to process them successfully. The different vantage point becomes problematic when one or both partners are not matching up to each other's expectations about the differences in intensity and time.

For example, the betrayed often expects the unfaithful to experience the same level of intensity they are experiencing: "Your intensity of guilt should match the intensity of my hurt and anger." This may not be possible, because, chances are the unfaithful has been feeling guilty since they started the affair, which may explain why their level of guilt after the betrayed finds out is less than what is expected. In addition to that, the unfaithful often feel a sense of relief once they are caught. Sometimes, that sense of relief tends to overshadow their feelings of guilt and shame, leading to the expression of a lesser intensity of emotions.

In another example, the unfaithful may be frustrated with the length of time it's taking the betrayed to process their feelings of hurt and pain. The unfaithful feel frustrated because they have been enduring the feelings of guilt for a long time and they are aching to end that suffering. From their perspective, it feels like the betrayed are taking too long to process their feelings. What the unfaithful are forgetting is that the knowledge of the affair is new to the betrayed, hence the appearance for needing more time. In reality, the time needed for both is usually comparable, but looks uneven because each has a different starting point.

What I encourage my clients to remember is to focus on the authenticity of the emotions exhibited by their partner rather than how closely it matches theirs. After all, both partners played different roles, at different points in time, which end up producing completely different experiences.

Emotional Burnout

The process of acknowledging the impact of infidelity is draining, because it takes an emotional toll on both partners. Many of my clients report having endless hours of heart-to-heart talks in which they've cried, yelled, and hugged out their feelings. Many times, couples start to feel emotional burnout and begin to worry about being in such a state.

My advice has always been for my couples to take frequent breaks in between those emotional talks to recoup. It's important to engage in self-care activities to ensure that the two of you are able to have the necessary energy to continue this journey. Be open about your burnout to avoid the misperception of being disengaged and disinterested. Give yourselves and each other the permission to take a break without beating yourself and each other up about it. But do it within reason and balance.

Support Reciprocity

What makes this milestone difficult is the fact that you and your partner are required to experience and share your feelings with one another about the affair. This act requires a high level of vulnerability, which is difficult to obtain even in the best of circumstances. What usually allows people to be vulnerable is safety, and what encourages them to sustain that vulnerability is support.

Acknowledging the impact of infidelity means that you are being asked to be vulnerable with the person who is the cause of your pain or the target of that pain, neither of which feels like a safe position to be in. Furthermore, it's difficult for the betrayed to accept support from the person who caused them pain, even if the unfaithful were more than happy and ready to offer it. It's also difficult for the betrayed to provide support for the unfaithful, even if they had the audacity to ask for it.

The difficulty in obtaining support from one another can deter a lot of couples from completing this milestone. This is why you and your partner should seek couples, individual, and group counseling to provide you with an appropriate outlet for support during these challenging times.

Urge to Punish

The need to punish is a universally shared human trait. Punishment is part of almost every culture that has ever existed since the beginning of time. We use it as a tool for enforcing justice and as a tool to shape behavior. This tool is utilized in almost every domain of our social interactions such as government institutions, religious ideologies, and family units.

The reason why the use of punishment has persisted to this day is due to our belief in its effectiveness in dealing with wrongdoings. But, most of us never really take the time to examine how and why punishment works and whether or not it's really the best way to deal with wrong doings.

I think we continue to use punishment because it allows us to accomplish two things. Firstly, it allows the victim to process the pain caused by the wrongful act. It does so by giving the victim a socially sanctioned way to reciprocate the pain he or she experienced, thus making things even, or just.

Secondly, it increases the prevention of future wrongdoings. This happens because we are naturally wired to avoid pain, and if we know that our actions have negative and painful consequences like feelings of guilt and shame, then we are more likely to avoid repeating such actions.

Infidelity is a wrongful act in which there is a victim and a perpetrator, thus warranting the need to discuss the role that punishment should play in the healing process. This is why we have to ask the important question, "What role does punishment play in the milestone of acknowledging the impact?"

Punishment is just like any other force that can be used for good or bad causes. The amount and timing of that force determines the effectiveness of its uses. When it comes to infidelity, punishment fails in being a constructive force when it's used for the wrong reason, the wrong amount, and the wrong time and duration.

I wish that there was a specific duration, type, and dispensing schedule of punishment that works for every couple, but such a thing does not exist. The general guideline, however, is as follows: punishment should only be used to help the unfaithful experience the natural consequences of his or her actions, no more, no less. When that goal is accomplished, there will no longer be a need for punishment to take place. What I emphasize to the betrayed is the "natural consequences" part. Meaning, there is no need for creating different ways to cause the unfaithful to suffer. The punishment should really come from the unfaithful's realization of the harm they caused the betrayed and the negative feelings that come along with that understating.

The common mistakes couples make when it comes to punishment is either they go too light or too heavy. If you shield your partner from experiencing the pain they should experience as a result of their behavior, they will not learn, because you are telling them there are no consequences for such acts. If you go out of your way to make your partner feel more pain than they deserve, then you miss the mark, and you destroy their desire and motivation for improvement. It's like the difference between justice and revenge. In summary, once punishment has served its purpose, couples need to make a conscious choice to move forward to rebuild.

Urge to Make Excuses

Nobody likes to know that they are in the wrong regardless of how valid that reality is. Our natural tendency when we are confronted with the realization that we made mistakes is to provide an explanation of the circumstances that led to those mistakes. These explanations are important and necessary to the healing process, but only if they are provided in the right time, and for the right reasons.

The mistake that the unfaithful often make is that they provided the explanation at the wrong time and for the wrong reason. You should never provide explanations before you acknowledge the impact of your mistake and provide an apology for it. Starting off with the explanation of why you made a mistake is usually perceived as an attempt at justification rather than an explanation.

Sometimes the unfaithful starts off with the explanation because they truly believe that this is what the betrayed wants to know; in other words, they are making an honest mistake. Other times, the unfaithful's motivation is really to provide rationalizations and excuses for their behaviors instead of actually owning up to their responsibility. The take-home message here is to choose the right time for providing the explanation, and do it in a way that still demonstrates accountability for your actions.

Urge to Rush the Process

The milestone of acknowledging the impact is a very painful process for both the unfaithful and the betrayed. The emotional energy required is high, and, at times, it overwhelms the couple causing them to want to cut the journey short prematurely because neither partner likes to suffer nor see their partner in suffering.

This is why you see both the unfaithful and the betrayed trying to go through this step quickly, or they try to avoid it all together. The end result is usually the illusion of a resolution versus actual resolve. Couples convince themselves that they allowed themselves to experience the full impact of the affair and then attempt to move forward to the next steps in the process. But, somehow, they find themselves stumbling because they suppressed a big portion of what they are feeling in the hopes of making it go away instead of actually giving themselves the necessary time required to get the job done.

I usually give the example of trying to put out a coal fire. The embers continue to glow bright underneath the surface long after you have put out the surface flames. If you want to truly move past this phase, allow it the necessary time it requires, so that once you are past it, you can leave it behind. Keep in mind that just because you completed this milestone doesn't mean that you and your partner will never have to discuss the impact of the affair again. This is based on the fact that there might be an unanticipated future impact. This means that the two of you have to be open to acknowledging future impacts as they surface.

Chapter 7

The Fourth Milestone:
Choosing a Path

"Know well what leads you forward and what holds you back, and choose the path that leads to wisdom."

---Buddha

Most couples consider this to be one of the most difficult milestones to complete, because it forces you to confront and resolve your ambivalence about the relationship. Those dealing with infidelity feel torn between ending and saving the relationship. This milestone will determine the future of your relationship, which makes it one of the most important steps in the healing process.

Despite the difficulty of this milestone, you and your partner can't afford to shy away from it. Avoiding or delaying its completion will ensure getting stuck. Being stuck at this juncture in the process can be very painful to experience and to witness. It's a unique kind of pain, because it's born out of the feeling of helplessness.

People feel helpless when they have no control over their future. It's hard to be in control when you know you are not taking the important steps needed to shape that future. Choosing a path allows you to take steps that will get you onto different grounds from the ones you already covered and experienced.

Why Do Couples Get Stuck?

When couples reach this point, they are already feeling exhausted because of the emotional energy spent completing the previous milestones. Furthermore, the significance of this milestone weighs heavily on the shoulders of the unfaithful and the betrayed, causing them to experience a lot of anxiety about taking action, especially since those actions could potentially lead to more pain and regret. Not knowing which path to choose and the fear of choosing incorrectly are the general factors causing one or both partners to get stuck. Here is a list of some of the common factors that cause couples to get stuck:

Fear of Making a Mistake

Couples worry about making a mistake because they are not sure about what they will find at the end of the path on which they embark. This is especially true when considering that both paths have the potential for pain, disappointment, and regret just as much as they have the potential for resolution, satisfaction, and happiness.

Taking the path of separation might protect the couple from having to re-experience the painful impact of infidelity because the risk of cheating on one another will be non-existent. But doing so, can also rob the couple from a chance for a happy, fulfilling relationship with one another. In this scenario, the fear of making a mistake stems from the desire to avoid the regret of giving up on something that had the potential for being wonderful.

Taking the path of rebuilding gives the couple an opportunity to make the positive changes needed to have an even happier and more fulfilling relationship than what they previously had. The success in achieving this has the added benefit of maintaining the family unit and increasing the couples' odds in overcoming future relationship conflicts. But taking this path does not provide protection against the potential for future pain and disappointment. This is based on the fact that you are choosing to be in a relationship in which infidelity already took place, thus the chances of it happening again are not beyond the realm of possibilities. In this scenario, the fear of making a mistake stems from the desire to avoid the pain associated with possible future incidents of infidelity.

Every decision we make comes with certain risks. That doesn't mean that we must avoid making decisions because of "what if's," nor does it mean that we should act blindly with complete disregard to consequences. The best thing to do is to make an informed decision based on calculated risks.

Now, calculating risks doesn't mean a 100% certainty of a particular outcome. Because, if that was the golden rule that we should use to reach any decision, then nothing would get done. A realistic calculation is one that focuses on choosing the path that has the highest percentage as the most likely outcome, even if it's as close as 51% to 49%.

Fear of Failure

This is another factor that is tied to the potential consequences that could come out of choosing either path. One of the main things stopping people from making decisions or taking action is the fear of failure. The power of that fear goes beyond our disappointment in ourselves to achieve a desired outcome. It extends to experiencing the negative results caused by such failure.

In the path of separation, couples worry about failing to survive the pain of separation and failing to move on with their lives. This is a valid fear, because having to end something you invested time and energy into is not easy, since it requires starting over from scratch somewhere else, which will have its own set of challenges. Separation is also a hard process to initiate and endure, because it impacts both partners and follows the same painful trajectory of the process of grief associated with loss.

In the path of rebuilding, the fear of failure is usually centered on the couple's abilities—the ability to endure the milestones of the healing process and the ability to make and sustain the changes in behavior. We are talking about a lot of changes — changes to heal, changes to prevent future affairs, and changes to make the relationship satisfying for both partners.

Making changes is not an easy process and it's normal for couples to worry about their ability to make and sustain the new changes. A lot of the changes needed are going to require learning new skills or exercising a muscle that's never been used, thus leading to concerns about success. At this point, I can give you my usual spiel about failure and how we should change our perception of it into a positive thing, because, in reality, it's a useful tool for learning.

The only problem here is that despite my belief in this spiel, I know there is no room for it when it comes to dealing with infidelity. It's easier to sell this idea of failure as a learning tool in situations with some wiggle room for failure. But when it comes to infidelity, the tolerance for failure is low, because the condition of the relationship is critical.

It's like the difference between a doctor making a mistake in treating a patient in ICU versus outpatient. Both mistakes will have negative consequences, but the ICU patient will have a smaller chance of recovery from that mistake.

So, instead of giving you this spiel, I will ask you to draw a line that both you and your partner can live with as tolerable and acceptable types of mistakes and failures that are suited to the critical condition of your situation. This is not a license or a permission to make mistakes and fail. It's simply a reality check to make you aware of the possibility for mistakes and certain types of failure that may take place. This reality check will help you see those types of mistakes and failures in perspective so that you won't use them as an excuse to abandon the path you choose.

You and your partner should also draw some hard lines on certain mistakes where there is no wiggle room, like sleeping with someone else while you are trying to work on your marriage. In addition to the hard lines, you and your partner should talk about your realistic expectations about the tolerable mistakes that can happen as a result of the process of learning new skills. Let's say that one of the changes being made is to be an attentive listener. One should expect that whoever is making that change might not be successful in every conversation or that their attentive listening ability is not going to be at 100% every time.

Bottom line, the possibility of making mistakes and failures exists in any path that you choose. There are acceptable, tolerable mistakes and failures that are associated with the learning curve and there are mistakes and failures that are caused by a poor calculation of risk.

If you don't choose a path, you are guaranteed to fail, simply because you are stuck standing still. But if you choose a path and walk it, you will actually have the potential for success.

Not Enough Information to Make a Decision

Choosing a path is one of the most important decisions that you will ever make in your life. It's a decision that can't be made on impulse. It should only be made after you analyze what took place in order to determine future outcomes. The information you will need to make that analysis comes from the milestones of "Getting the Story" and "Acknowledging the Impact." This means that you have to complete the previous milestones successfully in order to get the information you need to make this decision.

Couples get stuck when they skip previous milestones or conduct them poorly. This is why it's crucial for you and your partner to feel satisfied with the completion of each milestone before you move on to the next. It's hard for couples to choose a path if they still feel that the story of the affair is incorrect or incomplete. How can you be expected to make an informed decision without knowing the real story? It's also difficult to calculate the risks of each path if you and your partner fail to acknowledge the impact of the affair on your lives and whether or not you can move past that damage.

This is why I encourage my couples to be honest with themselves and each other when they can't make a choice because they need more information. If you don't identify what it is that you need from your partner in order to choose a path, you are going to be stuck and so is your partner. This is why I urge you to have an ongoing dialogue about your satisfaction of the amount and type of information that you both need in order to make a decision. You also need to be open to the idea of revisiting the previous milestones to assure that they were completed appropriately.

Fear of Sending the Wrong Message

This particular fear is often experienced by the betrayed who is leaning toward the path of rebuilding. The betrayed worries that the choice to rebuild will be misinterpreted by the unfaithful as, "all is well, and no more work is needed to get past the affair."

It's prudent for you and your partner to be cautious and calculating in regard to your words and actions to avoid misinterpretation of your intent, expectations, and where you are in the healing process. But choosing the path to rebuild doesn't mean that all is forgiven and that there is no need for more work and effort. It simply means that instead of standing at the fork in the road, you are making the decision to take a step in the direction of rebuilding. That means both you and you partner have to be extra clear about what taking that step means to each of you. So, yes, it's an important step, but it's not the end of the journey.

To overcome this fear, the betrayed needs to consider how failing to choose a path due to fear of sending the wrong message will impact the unfaithful. Because, from the unfaithful's perspective, they are following the correct steps to lead to the path of rebuilding, but somehow are not getting any results. This will cause them to feel discouraged, which in return will affect their motivation to continue working on themselves to heal the relationship. This becomes a self-fulfilling prophecy, because people usually give up trying when they feel that their actions are not getting them any closer to their goal.

Not Liking Your Options

Do you remember a time in which the options that were in front you were equally awful or at least seemed that way? If so, do you remember how that made you feel? Usually being in that predicament makes people feel helpless and hopeless because having what seems to be an equally bad option is often experienced as not having a choice at all.

These feelings of helplessness and hopelessness often lead to getting stuck. It goes something like this, "I don't like any of the choices in front me, so I am not going to choose." The interesting part about this is that refusing to make a choice is not going to magically remove the unpleasant options that we have on the table and replace them with better ones. Refusing to make a choice will only guarantee that a choice is going to be made for you and it would probably be the one that is the least in your favor, because you have chosen to relinquish control. Meaning, whatever force or person who has to make that choice is going to do so without your input.

When it comes to infidelity, sometimes the options of separation and rebuilding seem like equally difficult paths to take. This is based on the fact that both will require a lot of hard work and will involve a great deal of pain, with no guarantee of satisfaction. Regardless of this fact, couples should choose a path in order to get unstuck and move on with their lives.

Choosing a path will prevent you from prolonging your pain or suffering, because, when one or both partners refuses to choose a path, they are simply agreeing to be in the current painful emotional state which will persist until the couple finds a resolution. Being in that perpetual state of pain will eventually lead to separation. My advice is as follows: if that is the destination you want, then there is no need to get to it the hard way. If it's not what you want, then give the path of rebuilding a chance, because, after all, the option to separate will always be there if the path of rebuilding ends up leading to a dead end.

Fear of Selling Out

One the most devastating effects of infidelity is the creation of identity crises for both the unfaithful and the betrayed. When an unexpected event like infidelity takes place, it makes couples question their identity, because both partners will have their own ideas about how infidelity should be dealt with if it happens. Most people never imagined that they could be unfaithful or that they would be betrayed, therefore, they are ill-prepared to deal with infidelity when it actually happens.

The root of the identity crisis comes from the fact that the views the couple had about infidelity were based on what seemed like a far-fetched scenario, meaning that their ideas on how they might react to an affair were based on an imaginary event. Because the affair was not yet real, their ideas on how they might handle an affair tend to be nearsighted by nature, because they are based on a single dimension: the hypothetical.

When the affair actually happens, couples realize that the views they had about infidelity prior to the affair are difficult to stick to or act on. This is based on the fact that the way they actually feel now is different than how they thought they would feel during the hypothetical scenario.

Classic example, most betrayed say, "I always told myself, I would be gone if I ever found out that my partner cheated on me." This a common view shared by most people when asked about their reactions to a hypothetical scenario of infidelity. The reaction people give as an answer to this hypothetical is based on what they think they would feel if that far-fetched situation took place, which is most likely anger and pain. Why is it difficult, then, for these folks to act on the straight-forward, clear answer they provided in the hypothetical situation?

Because, when the affair actually takes place, the betrayed realizes the emotional experiences they are having are far more complicated than what they imagined it to be. It's true that they are feeling pain and anger which makes separating sound like the logical choice. But, they are also feeling the fear of making a mistake and the fear of giving up on something that can be fixed. These unanticipated feelings make it difficult to act on the views they previously had about infidelity prior to the affair.

The unfaithful also faces their own identity crisis struggle. A lot of unfaithful say, "I never thought I would put myself through the embarrassment and humiliation involved in trying to fix my relationship. I always thought that I would just leave if I had caused so much pain."

Once again the unfaithful's reaction in the hypothetical situation is based on how they imagine they would feel if they got caught cheating, which is embarrassment and humiliation, but when they are found out, they experience guilt and remorse in addition to the embarrassment and humiliation. These unanticipated feelings are what compels them to reconsider their reaction.

This conflict between what the unfaithful and betrayed thought they would do versus what they are actually considering doing after the affair makes them feel that they are selling out and not being true to themselves. This makes the couple question their identity and begin misinterpreting their new views about how they will deal with infidelity as a weakness of character.

Couples get stuck when they fail to resolve this incongruency. My job is to help them resolve that conflict by helping them understand the differences between selling out versus reevaluating. Selling out is doing things that you are not proud of because they are against who you are, but who you are is not a rigid and static concept that, once formed, is no longer open to change. Who you are in a hypothetical situation is not who you are in reality. Who you are is an ever evolving concept that should take into consideration your current state of being. In a nutshell, the conflicting emotions you are experiencing after the affair are really a reevaluation of your position in light of new information about yourself that you were not aware of when presented with the hypothetical situation.

***

The Choices You Have In front of You

There are three paths that are available for couples dealing with infidelity: rebuilding, separating, and undecided. The first two are the most common ones and will be discussed in more detail in future chapters. The third option is a little bit trickier, because in it the unfaithful is struggling on whether or not to end the relationship with the third party.

This usually manifests in two ways—one: the unfaithful is willing to put the relationship with the third party on hold while they work on their relationship with the betrayed; or two: the unfaithful wants to keep both relationships going at the same time to determine which one they would like to keep.

The first scenario falls under the path of choosing to rebuild because the unfaithful is focusing solely on rebuilding the relationship with the betrayed and manages to do so by completely ending their interactions with the third party. The second scenario is doomed for failure because the only thing the unfaithful is proving is that they want to have their cake and eat to, which means that their selfishness is going to suffocate any hope for rebuilding the relationship with the betrayed.

How to Choose a Path

We covered the significance of choosing a path as well as some of the factors that prevent couples from making that choice. Now it's time to go over the elements that you will need to help you choose a path. Think of these elements as the data that you will need to help you make an informed decision about the path that is most likely to yield the best outcome for you, your partner, and your family. Here are some of the elements you need to consider in making that decision:

Relationship History

The best way to examine this element is by asking the question, "How good was the relationship prior to the affair?" When couples seek counseling in general they fall into two categories: the had-it-and-lost-it category and the never-had-it-in the-first-place category. Both are fixable but have different game plans, as well as different probabilities for success.

The had-it-and-lost-it group are the couples who can recall a period of time in which both partners were satisfied and happy with the relationship on a consistent basis. But, somehow, life got in the way and forced the couple to drift apart. My job with these couples is to help them reconnect with the qualities that allowed them to feel that happiness and satisfaction and help them identify the issues that caused the drift between them. Once those issues are identified, I provide the couples with the tools they need to resolve these issues as well as tools they need for early identification of future problems so that they get addressed before escalation.

Couples in this category have a higher chance for success because they already had what they needed to make the relationship work once before, but just lost it along the way. The fact that they can recall a period of happiness and satisfaction gives them hope and motivation to do the hard work needed to rebuild.

The ones who never had it in the first place, are usually the couples who started their relationship on the wrong foot for a variety of reasons, such as the wrong motivation, poor knowledge of one's needs, and readiness for the relationship, etc. Usually those couples are hard-pressed to recall a time in which they were both happy with one another beyond the short period of dating. It's easy for couples to report satisfaction during the initial period of dating because everything is still new and everyone is presenting the best version of themselves to attract the other person.

My job with these couples is to help them unearth the real reasons they came together in the first place and help determine whether or not the two of them can recommit to each other for the right reasons. This process will involve rediscovering who they are as individuals and what they are looking for in a relationship. Once these things are identified, the two will have an opportunity to find out if they are able to match their expectations through appropriate compromises that allow the two to be happy and satisfied.

These couples have a lower probability in rebuilding because they don't have the element of optimism since there is no "relationship goodness" they can draw from. Furthermore, their learning curve for the skills they need to be happy is steeper, because they never acquired the skill in the first place. It's like you are asking them to achieve the same thing you are asking of the couples in the first category, but without having the optimism and the previous muscle memory.

Type of Affair

The next element to consider when deciding whether or not to rebuild the relationship is the type of affair that took place. The type of affair the couple struggles with plays an important role in influencing the paths they choose. In chapter two, we discussed the different types of affairs as well as other issues that lead to infidelity, such as mental illness, sex addiction, and sexual identity.

In the case of physical affairs, couples will need to evaluate their ability to fulfill each other's physical needs as well as their ability to overcome the insecurities caused by intrusive imagery and comparisons related to the affair. In emotional affairs, the couples will have to evaluate the extent and type of emotional attachment existing with the third party and whether or not those attachments will prevent the couple from rebuilding their emotional bond. In the mixed affairs, the couples will have to evaluate everything mentioned under physical and emotional affairs to calculate the risks associated with each path.

If the affair was caused by mental illness and sex addiction, couples need to be clear about what the mental illness or sex addiction means to the relationship, what the chances for recovery are, and they must evaluate their ability to endure everything that rebuilding will entail in terms of progress and setbacks. If the affair is due to sexual identity, couples need to explore the nature of the sexual identity and whether or not it will conflict with their worldviews or interfere with their ability to have a fulfilling and authentic relationship.

Actual Causes of the Affair

In choosing whether or not to rebuild the relationship, this element, the actual causes of the affair, is one of the most important sources of data used to help calculate the risk of each path. Identifying the cause of the affair will help you determine whether or not you and your partner are able to safeguard against future occurrences. In chapter three, we explored the main reasons that cause infidelity. Those factors were: never established a clear, agreed-upon contract in the first place; have a contract but one or both is not fulfilling their part; and the agreed-upon contract terms have never met the needs of one or both partners.

If the affair was caused by a lack of a clear, agreed-upon contract, then what you have to assess is your and your partner's ability to clearly identify your needs as well as your abilities to agree on how to fulfill these needs. Your success or failure in these domains will help you determine the risk associated with each path.

To assess the risks related to the affair caused by one or both partners failing to fulfill their part of the contract, couples need to evaluate their abilities to pinpoint the issues preventing them from sticking to their end of the deal. Once those issues are identified, couples need to demonstrate the ability to resolve them as well as the ability for early detection of future occurrences.

Lastly, if the affair happened because the agreed upon contract never met the needs of one or both partners, couples will have to reexamine their motivation and readiness for a committed relationship. If the right motivation and commitment is there, then they need to determine their abilities to live up to that motivation and commitment. The result of this assessment will help you calculate the risks associated with each path.

Performance During Previous Milestones

You and your partner's performance in the previous milestones is an important element in calculating the chances of success for each path. Completing those milestones tests two important ingredients that are needed for success: durability, and ability to make changes.

Durability is needed to help you see each path through to the end despite the challenges. Durability allows you to stay the course when things get tough, which they will no matter which path you choose. The previous milestones are intense emotionally and require a lot of endurance to complete successfully. Surviving those milestones is a measurement of durability.

Each path you choose will require the acquisition of new abilities needed to achieve healthy functioning. This means that you and your partner must demonstrate the ability to make changes. The previous milestones force couples to interact with one another in new ways that have never been experienced before. The couples who manage to complete those milestones successfully have proven their ability to make new changes in behavior.

Your success in completing the milestone of choosing a path will be contingent on two tasks: your ability to identify what's preventing you from choosing a path and the result of the risk and benefits analysis of each path you have in front of you. It's prudent to take the necessary and appropriate amount of time needed to accomplish these two tasks. Necessary and appropriate means don't drag your feet, but don't choose impulsively.

Chapter 8

The Fifth Milestone:
Creating a Plan of Action

"A goal without a plan is just a wish."

---Antoine de Saint-Exupery

Now that you and your partner have managed to choose a path, it's time to create a plan of action that will outline the steps needed to complete this path successfully. The first question I ask the couples who reach this milestone is, "What do you and your partner need to do in order to follow through with the path you have chosen?" The most common answer I get is, "I don't know," coupled with a blank stare and a shoulder shrug. Another variation of this answer is, "We just need time. Time heals everything."

The reason couples don't have a clear answer is because they are overwhelmed with the enormity of the task they chose to undertake. If you think about it, both rebuilding and separating are not easy, straightforward processes that you can complete overnight. Here, the couples are facing that old proverbial dilemma of, "How do you eat a whale?" The answer, of course, is, "One bite at a time." Meaning, despite the enormity of the tasks associated with the path you have chosen, you have to find a starting point to begin your journey, i.e., take a small bite. Once you complete that first step, you should be able to build another step on top of it until you eventually work your way up to the full completion of the path, i.e., eating the whole whale.

Another reason for the lack of a specific plan is caused by the couples' belief in the common myth we all grew up believing in, which is that time heals everything. Don't get me wrong; the passage of time does have a value in the healing process, but only if that passage of time was accompanied by action. Otherwise, twiddling your thumbs and waiting for time to heal you is simply a fool's errand. Time by itself is just the hands of a clock going in a circle, no more, no less. You need to come up with an action plan to get unstuck and use time as the medium needed to let this action plan produce its effects.

Prerequisites for the Plan of Action

I want you to think of the paths of rebuilding and separation as a major joint project that you and your partner are going to undertake to help you get unstuck. Every major project needs some prep work before an actual plan can be fully developed. The necessary prep work needed for starting this major project on the right foot requires obtaining the important prerequisites that are essential for creating the action plan. Those prerequisites are consensus of choice, clarity of motives, and expressed intent.

Consensus of Choice

In order for any joint project to be successful, the main players in that project have to agree on the actual project itself before they can create and implement a plan to complete it. This means that you and your partner must agree on which path to take before you come up with an action plan for that path. Failing to reach consensus of choice usually leads to a stalemate or false consensus that would eventually lead to sabotage.

Some couples are successful in obtaining consensus of choice, especially when they both come to the same conclusion about the risk analysis of each path. Other couples struggle in reaching a consensus because one or both partners failed to be objective in their assessment of risks or failed in taking the perspective of the other partner. This usually happens when one or both partners makes their decision solely based on their vantage point.

If you and your partner are struggling with reaching a consensus, I encourage you to make a conscious effort to recalculate the risk analysis to include both vantage points to assure the best chance for reaching an agreement. Be prepared that despite your best efforts to convince each other of your point of view, you may still end up with a disagreement.

If that is the final outcome, then the matter is already decided, meaning there is no other path to take besides separation, no matter how strongly the partner who wants to rebuild feels about his or her choice. In this scenario, the best thing to do is to accept the facts and work collaboratively to come up with an action plan of separation. Any attempts to twist arms, guilt trip, or pressure will only make things worse.

***

Clarity of Motives

An action plan for either path is going to require a commitment for a lot of difficult changes in behavior, thoughts, and feelings. Succeeding in making and sustaining those changes is what will allow you and your partner to complete the path you have chosen. One of the main causes of failure in making those changes is related to motivation.

Motives play a major role in our ability to succeed in making changes. Think of it as the fuel you need to allow you to stay the course. If you don't have enough fuel or the right kind of fuel, you will not be able to complete the path.

One of the common mistakes couples make is not being clear about their motivation for being on the path they have chosen. This lack of clarity is often caused by a lack of introspection (looking within), thus leading to a poor assessment of one's own motivations. Other times, the lack of clarity is self-inflicted. This happens when we choose to lie to ourselves about our true motivation in order to find a way to get what we want. Either way, the result of the lack of clarity leads to the same end of failing to make and sustain changes.

A classic example of wrong motivation for rebuilding the relationship is wanting to do so to keep the family unit intact. There is nothing wrong with desiring to keep the family unit intact, but that can't be the primary motivation for choosing to rebuild, especially if the risk analysis for rebuilding does not show that you and your partner have what it takes to rebuild.

Choosing to rebuild is a hard path to follow. The only way for couples to see it through is if they have the right motivation, which, in this case, should be the belief in each other's ability to make the relationship happy and satisfactory for both parties. Anything else short of that will not have the appropriate oomph or energy needed to sustain the changes required to complete this path.

You can't sacrifice relationship happiness just to keep the family unit intact. Even if you were able to do so, how much would you really enjoy this intact family unit when you are miserable in your relationship because neither you nor your partner has what it takes to make it satisfactory for each other?

An example of the wrong motivation to separate is to avoid the disappointment of failing to forgive or be forgiven for the affair. There is a difference between choosing to separate as a result of a thorough risk analysis of abilities versus choosing to separate to avoid a "what if" scenario.

The path of separation is equally difficult, and in order for the couple to complete it, they can't afford to battle with regrets. Regrets cannot be avoided if the couple's primary motivation for being on this path is based on the fear of uncertainty.

This is why you and your partner have to really assess your true motives for being on each path you choose. Making that assessment will help you find out if you are on the right path and whether or not you have what it takes to see it through. It's in everyone's best interest to be honest with yourself and each other about those motivations because at the end of the day the motivations are what will make or break your future.

Expressed Intention

Once you and your partner reached a consensus of choice and have identified the true motivations for the path you have chosen, you must express your intent to follow that path explicitly. This may sound silly to list as a standalone prerequisite, because, oftentimes couples feel that the intent to follow the path was implied through the other steps they have taken so far.

Expressing the intent is a major step and should be given the time and effort that is suited to its significance. Expressing your intention to follow the path is a declaration of commitment. An important declaration of this magnitude should be clear and explicit for both parties rather than left for guessing.

The power of outwardly expressing your intent comes from the fact that it provides you and your partner with a starting line for this joint project that the two of you are going to be working on. This means that it will force the two of you to make a conscious choice to focus your efforts on the future instead of dwelling on the past. This will increase your chances in making progress in your healing journey. Furthermore, having the conscious, clear, and agreed upon starting line can also be used as an accountability tool that will ensure that you and your partner are taking the needed steps to complete the joint project successfully without any delays or cutting corners.

Qualities of a Successful Plan of Action

Walking the path you and your partner have chosen is not going to be easy. This is why you need to develop the best action plan possible to help you see things through to the end. In addition to the completion of the above prerequisites, a successful plan of action must contain three important qualities: specificity, adaptability, and achievability.

Specificity

The fragile condition of the relationship after an affair does not leave any room for ambiguity. Every word and action counts, and so does every success and failure. A good action plan should be clear and tangible for both partners. The two of you should be crystal clear about the goals you want to accomplish and the specific steps you would like to see each other take to accomplish those goals.

Having vague goals and expectations will only lead to a miscalculation of your actual progress. Having agreed upon goals and measurable, concrete steps will allow you and your partner to gauge where you are in the path, which will allow for opportunities to make adjustments.

A vague goal can be something like, "I want us to be in love again like we used to be." This goal is vague because it's open to interpretation and does not offer concrete steps toward achieving it, which will make it difficult to measure progress.

A specific version of this goal can be something like, "I want to feel emotionally connected to you like I used to. What made me feel connected to you in the past was your desire and efforts in spending quality couple time together. " The phrase "quality couple time" could also be further specified; what does this time together entail to make it "quality time?" The specificity of this version of the goal allows the couple to shoot for the same reference point as well as provide each other with a guide for what steps to take to achieve that same reference point.

Adaptability

I have seen many well-thought-out plans fail simply because the couples who made those plans were rigid and closed off to change. Think of it this way: planning is usually based on what you believe is going to be true about a particular situation versus the actual situation itself in real life. This means that even the best-laid-out plans will require adjustment once they are put into action, simply because implementation may reveal some new unanticipated variable that the original plan didn't factor in.

When this happens, you have three options: soldier on and ignore the new variable, abandon the whole plan and call it quits, or revise the plan to factor in the effects of this new variable. Obviously the first two options will lead to a dead end. The first one will get you off course because you are choosing not to make the necessary adjustment to account for the new variable. The second will make you give up on a good plan, just because you didn't want to make adjustments. The third option is the only one that makes sense, because it will allow you to reach your final destination.

This means that you and your partner must create a plan that is flexible and adaptable to change. The two of you have to be willing and ready to modify your goals and the steps associated with them. Keep in mind that flexible should not be translated to wishy washy. There are fine lines between set-in-stone, open-for-change-when-necessary, and everything-goes. You want to be in the open-for-change-when-necessary category.

Achievability

Sometimes action plans fail because they lack realistic expectations. Having realistic expectations is crucial, because the success and failure of the action plan is solely based on the couple's ability to meet the agreed upon expectations. If the expectations are unrealistically high, the couple will feel discouraged because the goals they have outlined are unattainable, which leads them to abandon the path they have chosen. If expectations are unrealistically low, the couple won't feel any benefits from the goals accomplished because they are simply considered low hanging fruit and therefore won't produce value or a sense of progress.

For example, let's say the couple chooses the path of rebuilding, and one of the goals they want to achieve is rebuilding trust, and the measure of success in achieving that goal is to decrease the frequency of the betrayed's feeling of suspicion. Now, let's say that the number of times of feeling suspicious prior to the action plan is 10 times per week. An unrealistically high expectation would be expecting 0 incidents of feeling suspicious simply because you began implementing the action plan. If you set the bar too high, you are setting up your partner for an undeserved failure.

An unrealistically low expectation using that same example would be something along the lines of setting the goal for 9 or 8 times per week instead of 10. In this scenario, the impact of succeeding in meeting this low expectation will be minimal because its effects are not going to provide relief or a sense of progress.

Bottom line, you and your partner need to make an effort in developing a plan with realistic expectations of ability and time. It's also important to be able to distinguish the difference between realistic expectations and settling for less or pressuring for too much. Setting realistic expectations is adjusting the dial to match your abilities and to accommodate for the appropriate time needed to make new changes.

The Action Plan for Separation

If you are one of the couples choosing this path, then I am afraid that the last few pages in this chapter will mark the end of your journey with this book. But it's my duty to share with you the same advice that I give to all my clients. The path of separation and the path of rebuilding are equally difficult and have their own set of challenges, with one minor difference. The path of separation will drastically diminish any chances of rebuilding, if, for some reason, you change your mind in the future. So it's not a one-way ticket per say, but pretty darn close to it. The path of rebuilding, on the other hand, is not going to decrease your ability or chances for separation, if somehow you find out down the road that you and your partner are unable to rebuild.

Either way, I respect your decision and wish you the best of luck in completing your individual journey of healing. I would recommend that you read the rest of the chapters to see what the path of rebuilding involves. Now that we got this message out of the way, let's dive into the main components that the separation plan should include.

Intent and Closure

The plan of separation should start with the explicit declaration of the intention to separate. This intent should be clear and indisputable by both partners. Because, if you have reached this point, then you already know that there is no value in having a dissenting opinion, because at the end of the day, you can't rebuild a relationship with just one partner's interest. Expressing the intent to separate will provide you with the sense of resolution and finality needed to help you go on to the next steps

Closure is a process aimed at providing you and your partner with a summary of the sequence of events and factors that led you to the point of separation. This summary is designed to answer the questions, "Why are we separating, and did we do everything we can to avoid this point?" Closure is significant because it allows you to close the wound of separation in a way that is conducive to proper healing. It's a process that should not be taken lightly, because doing it poorly could further scar you and your partner. As I tell all my clients, "The only thing worse than ending your relationship is ending it with the wrong conclusion about why it had to end."

The benefit of having closure is that it allows you to move on without being hindered by doubts. Closure will also provide you with a laundry list of issues you would need to improve on to avoid making similar mistakes in future relationships. This is based on the fact that closure will outline what your mistakes were versus your partner's. This will help you avoid projecting the problems you experienced in this relationship onto future relationships.

The tricky part about providing closure is that couples mistake it for a last opportunity to set the record straight, which causes them to defend, attack, and blame. Other times, couples mistake closure as one more opportunity to change each other's minds about the decision to end the relationship. To me, closure is an opportunity for an objective reflection of how things got to this point. A well-executed closure is one in which couples manage to take responsibility and apologize for the part they played. It's also one that allows both partners to express their authentic emotional experiences about ending the relationship without blaming one another, because, if both have owned up to the part they played, there would be no need for the blame game.

When Do We Start?

When to start the separation is not an easy question to answer. Each relationship has its own unique set of complications and variables. This is why providing a one-size-fits-all answer is ill-advised. The "when to end" becomes a moving target based on each couple's needs and situation.

In a perfect world in which there are no shared responsibilities like kids, pets, finances, etc., the answer to the "when" question would be, "right away," or as soon as feasibly possible. Meaning, if each partner has the ability and the means to secure a separate dwelling, then they should separate once they develop and agree on the action plan. There is no need for delay, as long as you are able to separate while minimizing the damage and discomfort for everyone involved.

Sometimes couples get stuck on the "when," because one or both partners are trying to avoid the emotional discomfort of separation, so they make weak excuses to push back the date for the actual separation. Other times, couples get stuck because one or both partners feel guilty for causing the other partner pain as a result of the separation. Paradoxically these couples prolong their pain and suffering because they continue to avoid severing a tie that needs to be severed. My advice to you is, don't delay the start of the separation process to avoid the feelings of pain, guilt, sadness, and loneliness. Those feelings are part of the whole deal. The sooner you begin to experience them, the sooner you can process them and allow them to take their natural course.

How Do We Do It?

The specific logistics of each action plan is going to vary from one couple to another because of the uniqueness of each relationship. This is why I will focus on the general themes needed to guide those logistics. When you create an action plan for separation, you need to assure that the plan is fair and causes the least amount of damage.

Many couples struggle with being fair to each other during separation because of the hurt, anger, and pain they feel. But if couples have completed all the steps outlined in previous chapters, they will find themselves in a well-managed, emotional state that allows for the objectivity needed to be fair toward each other.

Furthermore, the way each partner views this step is going to dictate how successful they can be in being fair toward one another. If you see the plan of action to separate as an opportunity to hurt, punish, or guilt your partner, then you are not going to be fair. If you see the action plan for separation as your ticket to healing and putting this ugly business behind you, then you are going to succeed in being fair because your primary objective is to do what is best for you rather than trying to find the best ways to hurt your partner.

This is not the time to be selfish, nor is it the time to be a martyr. It's the time to choose what is going to be in your best interest as long as it does not rob your partner from their chances for happiness and satisfaction.

To ensure success in being fair and minimizing the impact of separation, I encourage my couples to seek mediation instead of litigation. Litigation is expensive, time consuming, emotionally draining, and has no guarantees of satisfactory outcomes. With litigation, you don't know the outcome of the separation agreement until a judge or jury decides who is right and who is wrong.

Mediation is becoming more popular and enjoys a higher rate of success and satisfaction, because it utilizes methods that make up for the shortcomings of litigation. You hire a neutral third party who does not judge the case but helps facilitate a discussion that will allow you to resolve your dispute amicably. It is less expensive, more confidential, and highly effective in resolving conflicts peacefully rather than with litigious court battles. Mediation helps in minimizing the impact of separation by allowing couples the opportunity to get things off their chests. The process also allows couples to see each other's point of view.

Future Interaction

Choosing the path of separation is a breakup process, meaning, you can have a clean breakup or a messy one. A clean break up translates to severing the ties and moving on with your life and avoiding crossing paths ever again. This is what I recommend for couples who have the luxury of not having shared responsibilities, like children, pets, finances, etc.

A good way to look at what kind of breakup you are going to have is by examining how you are going to redefine the relationship with your partner. Before the separation, you were a couple. After the separation, what are you going to be?

The complication comes into play when people fail to clearly define what roles they are going to play in each other's lives. The golden rule should be: no role in each other's future lives. Especially if there are no compelling reasons that would require you to be in each other's lives like kids who require co-parenting.

If your circumstances compel the need for being in each other's lives, then the role you play should be limited to what is necessary to fulfill your part in the task or responsibility you have in common.

For example, couples who share children often opt for co-parenting. The nature of the new roles should be limited to the scope of things needed to play that role successfully, no more, no less. In other words, you don't have to be each other's best friends and be involved in each other's lives in the same regularity you used to be prior to separation. All you need to do is be civil and kind toward each other as partners in parenting.

Couples who don't have kids or compelling reasons to be in each other's lives make the mistake of wanting to "stay friends." This almost always leads to future heartache and pain and makes the separation process messy. Friendships are built on intimacy. It's almost unavoidable to get that intimacy confused with the intimacy that used to be in the relationship as a couple. But even if couples managed to avoid that confusion, they can't avoid the feelings of resentment and anger about the ability to exist as friends but not as partners. Usually this leads to souring the friendship or setting up false hopes and expectations.

Long story short, can couples be friends after separation? Not very likely. A small percentage mange to do so, but often struggle with making it work. This is based on the fact that there are usually hidden motives for trying to maintain that friendship. Sometimes it's the fear of being alone, or the hope of reconnecting.

If you couldn't make it work as a couple, and you don't have a reason to compel you to be in each other's lives, the best thing to do is to move on and save yourselves and your future partners the pain that will come out of a friendship that is built on the wrong reasons.

Plan for Challenges

A major component of a good separation plan is preparing for the challenges you will face. As mentioned before, separation is a difficult process in which you and your partner will face many hardships. It's important for the two of you to anticipate some of those hardships and agree on the best ways for handling them.

For example, couples often struggle with feeling sad and lonely during the early phase of separation. In such times, couples may feel compelled to reach out and reconnect, which will feel like the right thing to do because that is the only thing they can think of to make the loneliness and sadness go away. But most likely, reconnection will lead to more pain and heartache because you will either be faced by rejection or a temporary acceptance that will end with regret.

A good action plan is to anticipate those feelings and have agreed upon ways for dealing with them in a way that is conducive for successful completion of the separation process. Using the previous example, the couple can share with each other their concerns about facing that hardship and brainstorm healthy solutions to deal with it, like surrounding one's self with family and friends, or staying busy and productive to minimize the impact of the feelings of loneliness and sadness.

The Need for Support

Once again, separation is going to be difficult and you will reach a point in which you will not be able to support one another because you are going to be physically and emotionally separate. This is why your action plan should include a reliable personal and professional support system that can help you stay the course.

This is the time to seek support from family, friends, and community. You don't have to do it alone, and there is nothing wrong with seeking support. You were there for your friends, family, and church, so now it's time that they were here for you. Don't see asking for support as a burden. See it as a privilege that you bestow on others to be there for you in difficult times. Believe it or not, people feel good about themselves when they know that they are able to help their loved ones.

I also encourage my couples to seek individual counseling during this time. Ending a relationship often makes people feel lost and confused. Individual counseling will give you the space to reorient yourself and rediscover and rearrange your priorities. This will help you plot out the future course of your life, which will allow you to prepare for that next phase.

Many couples make the mistake of jumping into another relationship right away. They do it for a variety of reasons like revenge, getting attention, avoiding loneliness, and so on. Individual counseling will help you make the right decision about future relationships by helping you discover what you want, why you want it, how to get it, when to get it, and your overall readiness for it.

The Action Plan for Rebuilding

When couples choose the plan to rebuild, they often do so with a great deal of apprehension and uncertainty. It's normal for you to be apprehensive, because you are not sure whether or not you and your partner are going to be successful. Some couples also struggle with the thought of, "what if this doesn't work? This whole thing would have been a waste of time."

What I tell my clients who are opting for the path of rebuilding is, even though there is a chance for failure, that doesn't mean that the work you have invested in rebuilding is a waste of time. The investment in rebuilding, despite the end result, buys you and your partner a very important thing. That thing is the peace of mind that comes from knowing you did everything within your power to save your relationship. This will prevent you from struggling with future regrets if you end up separating after an unsuccessful attempt to rebuild. That peace of mind is what makes this choice a worthy endeavor.

For the record, I have the utmost respect and admiration for the couples who opt for this path. This is based on the fact that they are putting themselves out of their comfort zone despite their hesitation. They are attempting to overcome many great challenges with minimum guarantees. This is why it's important for you and your partner to put a great effort in crafting the best action plan to ensure you are successful, especially when considering the level of investment you are agreeing to put forth.

Once again, since each relationship is unique, I am going to offer you the general themes needed to guide you in creating your own specific action plan. Your plan should include the following components:

Intent and Disclosure

Because of the significance of expressing intent discussed earlier, it should be the starting point of your action plan. The explicit expression of the intent to rebuild will assure that you and your partner are on the same page, as well as provide a starting line that can be used to gauge your future progress. It's important to draw that starting line clearly to make sure that you and your partner are holding each other accountable for future actions instead of past ones. This will assure the accuracy of your measurement of success and failure.

The complete action plan to rebuild is going to serve as a binding contract between you and your partner. This contract will outline the expectations you have of yourself and each other as well as your responsibilities toward yourself and each other. So, it only makes sense to have a proper disclosure take place before you start drafting this contract.

Disclosure is the process of revealing what's hidden. As far as disclosure within the context of the action plan, it's the process of revealing anything that you and your partner should know as it pertains to your ability to meet each other's expectations in the action plan. Here, disclosure should include your level of willingness, abilities, and concerns about potential obstacles. Discloser should also include your true motivations for wanting to rebuild. Those motivations can't be general statements like, "I want to rebuild, because I love you." Those motivations have to be very specific and concrete instead of empty words of optimism. An example of clearly stated motivation is, "I want to rebuild because we used to have the ability to satisfy each other's needs, and I think that we have what it takes to make each other happy again, and here is why…."

Lastly, disclosure should also include an explicit understanding and agreement to the risks that are associated with this path as well as the commitment for putting forth the time and effort needed to complete the path successfully.

When Do We Start?

With the action plan to rebuild, the only answer is now. There is no later. The longer you wait to rebuild, the more complication you create for yourself and your partner. When time lapses with no action, it creates ambiguity of expectations which is a setup for failure. This is based on the fact that couples misinterpret a lack of action as a sign of a lack of interest and dedication versus seeing it for what it is, which is not having a clear plan to follow.

The plan to rebuild should be implemented as soon as it's completed. This means that the door to the third party should be completely closed off while you are creating and implementing the action plan to rebuild. The last thing that you and your partner need is the interference of a third party. When you are choosing to rebuild, you are choosing to focus all of your attention and effort on that process. This means that this should be your main priority and you need to rearrange your life to make it so. This is why you need to make sure that you are carving out the time, energy, and resources needed to create and implement this plan successfully.

How Do We Do it?

The plan to rebuild will be comprised of your expectations of one another to achieve the outcome of satisfaction and happiness with the relationship. Those expectations are going to vary from one relationship to another, but they should all include the same major components. To ensure the success of this plan, it must be developed in a way that ensures clarity and tangibility. Meaning, you both have to be crystal clear on your understanding of your expectations of each other and those expectations must be concrete and tangible to allow you to measure success. Your action plan should be crafted in a comprehensive way that will include clear goals, concrete steps to achieve those goals, and indicators to measure success and failure.

Clear Goals

You will need to develop two sets of goals. Short-term goals and long-term goals. The short-term goals should be focused on rebuilding trust and earning forgiveness. The long-term goals should be focused on fixing the relationship problems that led to the affair. Keep in mind that the label of short-term and long-term should not be mistaken for chronology of order. Meaning, you will be working on both sets at the same time; you are just putting more emphasis on the short-term goals in the beginning, then shifting that emphasis to the long-term goals when the short-term is nearing completion.

Short-Term Goals: Trust and Forgiveness

Both of these goals will require concrete actions as well as time to accomplish them. You and your partner must identify healthy, realistic, and measurable steps to achieve these goals. Trust will need to be rebuilt in both directions. The betrayed needs to get to a point in which they can trust that their partner won't stray, and the unfaithful needs to get to the point in which they trust that their partner won't be invading their privacy to look for signs of wrongdoings.

When you begin to set the expectations of one another in regard to the issue of trust, I want you to consider what trust actually means. The reason it's important to define it, is because you and your partner need to agree on what that means to the two of you. Furthermore clarifying that definition will allow you to avoid setting up unhealthy steps to achieve trust.

Trust is a concept that is similar to faith in the sense that it's something that should be self-evident rather than something that needs to be constantly proven through surveillance and monitoring. Think of it this way: the people who believe in God do so even though they have never seen or heard God. But despite the lack of visual or auditory evidence of God's existence, they still firmly believe. They manage to do so because they utilize logic and reasoning to support their belief instead of looking for tangible physical evidences. This fact is what makes faith a powerful and persistent force, because it doesn't get its energy form sensory data that are often open to misinterpretation and corruption.

The reason why trust should be treated similarly to the concept of faith is based on the fact that doing it any other way will be missing the point. Because, one: there is no way for you to see and hear everything that your partner is up to; and two: even if there was such a thing, it would be a full-time job that changes the dynamics of the relationship from romantic partners to a parolee and a parole officer, neither of which is an enjoyable role to play.

The healthy thing to do is to build the trust on logic and reason, which means that you need to put your effort in addressing the issues that caused the affair in the first place as well as the factors that prevented you from fixing those issues. If you succeed in achieving this, then logic will dictate that there is no longer a reason for the unfaithful to cheat again.

When it comes to forgiveness, it's noteworthy to mention that it goes beyond the betrayed forgiving the unfaithful. It should also extend to the unfaithful forgiving themselves. It's something that should be earned rather than expected. A lot of couples struggle with figuring out how to earn and when to grant forgiveness. I wish there was a specific answer that could work for every situation, but unfortunately such a thing does not exist.

What I can offer you instead is the understanding of how forgiveness should be obtained. The process of seeking forgiveness involves conscious efforts to make up for wrongdoings. It's also a process that involves efforts of redemption, which means to make things better or acceptable. These efforts should serve as an indicator of learning from past mistakes, which can only be accomplished if supported with action that reflects learning from your past mistakes.

You and your partner will need to identify what actions you need to see from yourself and one another that can make up for the wrongdoing and that can change things back to an acceptable point. Once that's accomplished, then forgiveness can be granted.

It's important for couples to avoid mistaking the process of redemption and making up for wrongdoing with bribing. This means that the actions needed to achieve forgiveness have to correlate to the wrongdoing for which you are seeking forgiveness and redemption. For example, buying your partner an expensive gift is a bribe and not an act of redemption. This is based on the fact that buying a gift doesn't demonstrate learning from the mistake you made and it does not demonstrate changes in behavior.

Long-Term Goals: Fixing the Relationship Problems that Led to the Affair

This is the part where you and your partner will have identified the areas of relationship dissatisfaction that led to the affair. In addition to those issues, you have the opportunity to assess all the different areas of the relationship that need improvements. The goal here is not to just prevent future affairs, but also to assure the overall happiness and satisfaction in the relationship. I always give the analogy of rebuilding a home after it's been totaled by a hurricane. Now that you have the opportunity to rebuild from scratch, why not rebuild it to be your dream home instead of making a copy of what it was before the affair.

The best way to set up your long-term goals is by evaluating every aspect of your interaction as a couple no matter how big or small. In addition to the evaluation of the areas of interaction that contributed to the affair, you should also evaluate the aspects that you believe are working well because you never know what you will find out until you actually make that assessment. Some of the major areas I ask couples to evaluate are things like communication skills, co-parenting, division of labor, emotional connection, sexual compatibility and satisfaction, and supporting each other in achieving individual and relationship goals. This is not a comprehensive list, but it should point you in the right direction.

Concrete Steps and Measurable Indicators

Once you identify the clear, short and long-term goals, you will need to develop and agree on the specific concrete steps each one of you is going to take to achieve those particular goals. If these steps are not concrete and tangible, it will be difficult for you to assess how successful you are in achieving these goals. Once the concrete steps are identified, you need to develop reliable indicators that you can use to measure the progress or lack thereof. These indicators will be the accountability tool for both of you to assure that you follow through with what you promised to deliver. Those indicators will also allow you to make the necessary adjustments in steps, if somehow you both feel that you are not achieving your goal, despite your best efforts in sticking to the action plan.

Identifying concrete steps means having to state expectations from one another. Some couples are not comfortable with the idea of stating expectations. One source of discomfort is the fear of a lack of sincerity behind the actions, "If he does it because I expect him to do it, then its meaningless."

Expectations should not be seen as obligations. It simply means that you are telling your partner what you need from them rather than leaving them in the dark. Keep in mind that your partner has the option to agree or disagree to honor your expectation. That power of choice takes away the obligation. People need direction, especially if you want them to succeed. The need for direction is even more important when dealing with infidelity, because sometimes the unfaithful comes across as indifferent when in fact he or she is not taking actions, because they don't want to make things worse.

Another reason why some couples are uncomfortable with stating expectations is the worry about coming across as bossy, demanding, or needy. What I try to emphasize is that expressing your needs does not negate the balance of equality in the relationship. Stating your expectations is merely stating what currency you accept to achieve a specific outcome.

Goal Setting Example

Clear Goal

Let's say you and your partner believe that you need to improve how the two of you communicate with one another, and now it's time to set a long-term goal. Before you do that, you must clearly specify what kind of communication problems you have instead of setting a general goal of, "I want to improve my communication."

Communication problems are many and are caused by a variety of reasons. This means that you have to hone in on the specific communication problems the two of you are struggling with. Let's say that you ask that question and the answer you come up with is, "Our communication problem is misinterpreting each other's words." Now your clear goal will be, "I want to avoid or minimize the number of times in which we misinterpret each other's words."

Creating Concrete Steps

The best way to identify concrete steps toward achieving your goal is by identifying the specific cause of the problem. You have to ask, "Why do we misinterpret each other's words?" So, let's say the answer you come up with is, "We misinterpret each other's words because we don't think about what we are trying to convey before we open our mouths and speak."

Now that you have identified the specific problem and what caused it, you will be able to create concrete steps to fix it.

Step 1 (prevention): "We will both take the time to think about what we are trying to convey before we speak. Once we do that, we will take the time to choose the right words that will help us deliver that message successfully."

Step 2 (intervention): "Whenever my partner says something that rubs me the wrong way, I will take the time to tell him or her what I think they are trying to convey by saying something like, 'This is what I think you are trying to convey to me, but I am not quite sure, so did I hear you correctly?' " Making this statement will give you and your partner an opportunity to clarify what you are trying to say.

Developing Measurable Indicators

The indictors for success should be tied to the future frequency of the problem as well as the frequency of adhering to the steps outlined above. Your indicators of success will be based on the decrease or increase of the incidents in which you and your partner misinterpret each other's words. So, you need a baseline to compare progress to.

Let's say prior to taking the steps outlined above you and you partner misinterpreted each other's words 7 times per week. Now you must shoot for a realistic target new baseline as an indicator of progress. You also need to shoot for a reasonable timeframe for reaching that new baseline. So instead of saying, "A week from now we want to be at 0 incidents of misinterpreting each other's words," you should shoot for something realistic like, "A week from now we should have no more than 3 incidents of misinterpreting each other's words." The end game is to continue to make progress until you are no longer having that problem, or at least have it once in a blue moon.

Your action plan is going to be one of the main tools you will be using to help you complete the path you have chosen. This is why it needs to be crafted in a way that will achieve satisfaction for you and your partner. In order for this tool to be useful, it needs to be relevant to your desired goals as individuals and as a couple. Once crafted, it will need to be put into action. Implementing the plan will allow you to determine its effectiveness and whether or not it needs modification, which will be discussed in the next chapter.

Chapter 9

The Sixth Milestone:
Implementation and Healing Pains

"Healing doesn't mean the pain never existed. It means the damage no longer controls our lives."

---Akshay Dubey

Now that you have the action plan in place, it's time to begin implementation. In this milestone, you and your partner will prove to yourselves the ability to make the changes you have promised. This is a monumental task that can overwhelm couples due to the pressure associated with the fear of failure. This is why I will give you the same rules that I give to all my clients to assure that the implementation phase is done successfully. Following these rules will assure that you stay on track and make the necessary adjustments needed to complete your path.

Rule #1 Stick to the Plan

The reason I ask my clients to spend so much time creating a concrete plan is because they need to use it as a map for the path they are on. It doesn't make any sense to spend all of this time creating a map that you are not intending to follow. A lot of couples make the mistake of sticking to the plan for the first few weeks, then they decide to "wing it" the rest of the way and somehow hope to arrive at their destination.

This is not the time to improvise or switch things around willy-nilly, especially when there is so much at stake. If there's a need to modify the goals and the steps outlined in the plan, then make those changes together after thoughtful consideration and discussion. Sometimes one or both partners make a solo decision on how a specific goal should be met in a way that is different from what was agreed upon in the action plan. They do so with the best of intentions thinking that this is what their partner wants as well. But, often times, these changes get interpreted as a lack of compliance with the agreement rather than a noble attempt to go above and beyond to meet a goal.

Rule #2 Show Your Work

The main goal of the action plan is to prove that you and your partner are capable of making the needed changes to heal from the affair and rebuild your relationship. This is why your effort to complete the steps and accomplish the goals outlined in the action plan is going to be the measurement of your success and failure.

Your success in making those changes should be visible and noticeable to one another. Because, if your partner is not able to see that you are putting forth the effort, he or she will start wondering whether or not they should put in the effort as well.

Often times, one or both partners make the mistake of not showing their efforts. This usually happens for two reasons—one: the person is actually not making an effort, and that's why they are not able to show it; or two: the couple failed in creating measurable indicators of progress to achieve the goals in the action plan. This is why I emphasize the importance of coming up with agreed upon indicators that would reflect success in making the changes outlined in the action plan. Those indicators should reflect changes in thoughts, feelings and action.

For example, if one of the changes expected for one partner is to be less selfish, then I would need to see that they are thinking of others needs before making a decision (change in thought). I would also need to see that they are able to feel guilty if they find out that their selfishness is going to impact others (change in feelings). Lastly, I need to see that they are able to take actions and make decisions that are based on what is in the best interest of everyone instead of just themselves (change in action).

Rule #3 Avoid Misperceptions

The fact that this milestone is a true test of your abilities and potential for success makes it very important to avoid misperceptions. The biggest misperception that you want to avoid is your dedication to the plan. Lack of dedication is an indicator of failure to make change and that failure translates to doubts about future relationship satisfaction.

Misperception of dedication usually happens when one or both partners are struggling to follow through with one or more of the expectations they agreed to, but instead of talking to their partner about their struggle which would allow for problem solving, they keep that struggle to themselves and end up not delivering what they promised.

The reason behind the struggle to meet expectations can either be valid or not. But, if you don't address that struggle, you will miss out on the opportunity to fix the problems. So, if you are struggling to meet an expectation because of obstacles, seek help. If you are struggling because you are confused about an expectation, then ask for clarification. If you are struggling with an expectation because it's unrealistic, then have a dialogue with your partner to readjust, but don't wait to the last minute before you say something to your partner. The best way to avoid misperceptions is by clear and timely communication. Talk to your partner about the difficulties you are having in meeting expectations before your deadlines rather than after the fact. Think of it this way: valid reasons behind the inability to meet expectations will turn into lame excuses if you share those reasons after the fact. It's all about timing.

Rule #4 Assess Your Progress

The most important part of implementation is the regular assessment of your progress. The benefit of doing this is three-fold—one: it gives you hope and motivation to stay the course; two: it will ensure that each progressive step you complete is built on a solid foundation; and three: it gives you an opportunity to make the necessary adjustments for unanticipated variables.

The assessment of your progress should be done individually and as a couple and it should happen on a consistent, agreed upon frequency. This means that you and your partner should schedule a daily or weekly check-in time in which you both share your thoughts about your own progress, the progress of your partner, and the effectiveness of the action plan.

The check-ins should not be used as an opportunity to beat each other up and make each other feel bad. It should be used as an opportunity to celebrate successes, highlight efforts, and pinpoint areas for improvement. It's not a supervisor doing an employee evaluation; it's two partners reviewing the progress of their company in a collaborative, non-punitive fashion.

Rule # 5 Reevaluate and Make Adjustments

This particular rule is a reminder for the need to exercise adaptability during the implementation phase of your action plan.

This means that whatever feedback and information you get from one another from your regular check-ins should be utilized to make adjustments to the action plan.

The scope of that adjustment should include modifying goals and steps that are not working as well as including new goals and steps that need to be added as a result of new variables. The two aspects that you and your partner should think about prior to making any changes are the rationale behind the change and the timing of it.

Make sure that you have a really good reason to make the change, and make sure that you have given the preexisting plan adequate time to do what it's supposed to before making the decision to make any changes. Also make sure that the changes are agreed upon by the two of you.

Rule # 6 Be Patient and Empathetic

Implementing the action plan is going to be an arduous process, especially when considering that the two of you are going to be exercising new muscles and learning new ways of thinking, feeling, and behaving. You need to be supportive of one another during this phase as well as understanding of the difficulties that are associated with implementing the action plan. Being understanding and supportive doesn't mean allowing for and making excuses for failure; it simply means that you need to look at the big picture when you are evaluating you and your partner's overall success.

The two qualities that are helpful during this time are patience and empathy. You need to be patient with yourself and your partner about how quickly you are achieving your goals and the amount of struggle associated with this process. You also need to be empathic to where your partner is emotionally, and how their emotional state is impacting their ability to follow through with the expectations they have agreed to. Again, being patient and empathetic doesn't grant permission to fail or slack off. It merely means that you need to take everything into consideration before you come to the conclusion of failure or lack of dedication.

***

Healing Pains

In this section we are going to cover some of the anticipated healing pains that you and your partner may experience during the implementation phases of the action plan. It's very important to understand that the issues contributing to these pains should not be seen as indicators of the failure of the action plan. Healing pains are the residual effects of the affair that need to run their course. Think of them like the last few days of a flu cycle; yes, you no longer have the chills, fever, and muscle aches, but now you are dealing with a lingering fatigue and a sore throat from all that coughing.

The reason I am asking you to make the distinction between the healing pains and the challenges associated with implementing the action plan is to maintain objectivity and to prevent miscalculating your successes and failures. Keep in mind that the list of healing pains described below is not conclusive, and may not be applicable to every couple. It's a list of the most common healing pains experienced by the majority of my clients.

Healing Pain of Post Affair Stress Disorder

Infidelity is a major traumatic event that causes many residual effects that impact both the unfaithful and the betrayed. It's common for couples to be afflicted by some of the same symptoms displayed by individuals healing from traumatic events like war and assault. The betrayed is usually the one who exhibits the bulk of these symptoms. The unfaithful is usually impacted by the effects of those symptoms on the relationship and the progress of the entire healing process.

Victims of infidelity share some of the common symptom criteria exhibited by individuals who are diagnosed with Post Traumatic Stress disorder. The first criterion is the persisting re-experience of the traumatic event. The second criterion is the avoidance of the trauma related stimuli. The third criterion is negative thoughts and feelings that begin to worsen after the trauma.

The fourth criterion is increased reactivity and hyper arousal that begins to worsen after the trauma.[9]

The persisting re-experience of the traumatic event usually manifests through intrusive thoughts and images about the affair details. These are negative thoughts and images that are unwanted, yet somehow force their way into your head. Another way this criterion manifests is through having nightmares about the affair and future incidents of its reoccurrence. Other symptoms include flashbacks to the vivid memories of finding out about the affair. Those flashbacks can be triggered either by emotional and physical reminders of the affair or by things that are not directly related to the affair.

The avoidance of the trauma related stimuli after the affair usually manifests through conscious and subconscious efforts to avoid thoughts and feelings related to the affair. This usually takes place when one or both partners attempts to avoid talking about the affair, or tries to escape the negative feelings about the affair by trying to rush the healing process. Another common expression of this symptom criterion is the attempt to get rid of any reminders of the affair. This could be something as simple as buying a new bed or as elaborate as selling a house or switching jobs, leaving town, etc.

As for the negative thoughts and feelings that begin to worsen after the trauma, this usually manifests through overly negative thoughts about the self and the world, "I must be so naive," or, "No one can be trusted. Everyone cheats." Another symptom is the exaggerated blame of self and others for causing the affair. This is not the healthy, appropriate type of blame. This is solely putting the blame on one party who may have played a part, but should not be held responsible solely for the affair. "This is all my fault. If only I was a better wife, this wouldn't have happened," or "This is entirely his fault. She wouldn't have strayed if he hadn't been flirting with her." Lastly, this symptom criterion can manifest through an overall state of negative emotions and the associated behaviors that are caused by these emotions. Couples usually experience sadness,

---

[9] American Psychiatric Association: Diagnostic and Statistical Manual of Mental Disorders, Fifth Edition. Arlington, VA, American Psychiatric Association, 2013. Pages 271-274

anxiety, and difficulty in experiencing pleasure. This usually leads to a sense of loneliness, decreased desire for pleasurable activities, and isolation.

In regard to the fourth criterion of increased reactivity and hyper arousal that begins to worsen after the trauma, it usually manifests through four major symptoms. The first one is irritability and aggression. This takes the form of having a shorter fuse than usual and having a hyper sensitivity to things that you used to have a higher tolerance for.

The second symptom is risky and destructive behavior such as substance abuse, speeding, gambling, and so on. Those behaviors are born of out an apathetic attitude, in which people feel that they already lost the most important thing in their life, so nothing else matters.

The third symptom is difficulty concentrating and sleeping. This is usually the result of the emotional and cognitive fatigue caused by dealing with the affair. It's hard to concentrate and sleep when there are a lot of things on your mind.

The fourth symptom is hyper vigilance, which means an increased state of sensitivity geared toward detecting future threats to avoid future trauma. Think of it this way: if you were bitten by a snake when you were out hiking, the next time you go out for a hike, you are going to be ultra-aware of your surroundings to avoid getting bitten again. This ultra-awareness is exhausting, because it requires living in a perpetual state of anxiety. This means that you are on guard all the time to prevent future pain. Add to it the fact that you are not going to be just looking out for snakes but also anything that resembles a snake. This means over reaction to non-threating stimuli just to avoid future pain.

The way this plays out in couples dealing with infidelity is that you will see the betrayed reacting intensely to things that did not used to bother them before. For example, a person who didn't have any issues with their partner having innocent, appropriate interactions with co-workers of the opposite sex before the affair, will now have a different anxiety-based reaction to any interaction between their partner and all others of the opposite sex in any setting no matter how innocent and appropriate those interactions are.

Another example of hypervigilance can be seen in the betrayed's preoccupation with the whereabouts and the interactions of the unfaithful at all times. This often translates into the need for constant monitoring like GPS tracking and/or frequent checks by hacking emails, texts, and phone records. All of these efforts are motivated by the desire to avoid future pain. The logic usually goes something like this, "If I am watching every step, I am less likely to get tricked again."

The PTSD symptoms caused by the affair are unpleasant, but they are not eternal and can be overcome if you follow your action plan. The more successful you are in rebuilding the relationship and fixing the issues that contributed to the affair, the more success you will be in overcoming these symptoms. In addition to following the action plan, I urge couples to seek individual and couples counseling to help in the management of these symptoms. I also encourage couples to be understanding and patient with one another as it pertains to the impact of these symptoms on their overall functioning. Meaning, now that you know what to expect and why it happens, cut yourself and your partner some slack and come up with ways to ease the burden of these symptoms. Don't enable the symptoms, but understand and accommodate for them while working on a resolution.

I also urge couples to avoid making any rash, big decisions about relocation and selling homes. This is based on the fact that there is no way to erase all reminders of what took place. At the end of the day, you are choosing to rebuild the relationship with your partner who is a reminder of the affair that you can never get rid of. So don't be hasty. Solve the real problem by following your action plan. Getting rid of reminders will only provide temporary relief. Once trust is restored and the relationship is rebuilt, the symptoms of the Post Affair Stress Disorder will dissipate.

Healing Pain of Physical Intimacy

Resuming and reestablishing the physical connection between couples after an affair has many challenges. This is based on the fact that infidelity creates emotional and physical barriers that prevent couples from resuming and rebuilding their physical intimacy. Furthermore, for some couples, the lack of physical or emotional intimacy was one of the main factors that contributed to the affair, which means that in order for them to regain the physical intimacy, they must fix the barriers that have nothing to do with the affair, as well as the ones that are caused by it. My focus in this section will be on the emotional and physical barriers caused by the affair.

Emotional Barriers

One of the emotional impacts of infidelity is the feelings of insecurity. The betrayed usually starts to question whether or not they are good enough or attractive enough for their partner. That feeling of insecurity is usually coupled with the feelings of anger and resentment toward the unfaithful who is causing all of this insecurity. All of these negative feelings make it difficult for the betrayed to want to engage in any kind of sexual activities.

Furthermore, one of the symptoms caused by the trauma of infidelity is the reoccurring thoughts and images related to the affair. Usually, the betrayed is struggling with intrusive thoughts and images of their partner having sex with the third party. Those thoughts and images produce feelings of disgust and anger which make it difficult to want to have sex, especially when considering that doing so will trigger more of these thoughts and images.

Another emotional barrier is the trap of making comparisons. This is a product of insecurity as well as the intrusive thoughts and images. The betrayed struggles with having to compare themselves with the third party. The betrayed is torn, because he or she wants to make their partner happy to avoid future affairs, but also feels resentful that they are having to change who they are sexually based on what made the third party appealing to the unfaithful. In this scenario, the need for comparison will either result in underperforming or over performing in reference to the previous level of sexual activity prior to the affair.

The impact of the need for comparison makes the unfaithful uncomfortable about expressing their sexual likes and dislikes, because they want to avoid hurting the betrayed's feelings. The unfaithful worries that expressing their sexual likes and dislikes will lead to the unavoidable push of the comparison button.

Another emotional barrier is the struggle to identify the true motivation for wanting to resume physical intimacy. Often, couples feel compelled to engage in sexual activities amidst the process of healing from the affair. This usually happens because a lot of the milestones in the healing process require a high level of vulnerability and intimacy, which is often accompanied by the desire to be physically intimate.

In other words, sometimes sex happens because couples are feeling emotionally close. The struggles come up when the betrayed is conflicted about their motivation to be physical. Sometimes the betrayed feels that having sex is a copout or that it's sending the message of, "All is well and everything is forgiven." Other times, the betrayed worries that they are having sex out of fear and obligation because they know that their partner has physical needs that must be met, and they don't want them to go without sex to avoid future affairs.

My advice to my clients is to avoid resuming sexual activities until they feel that they are both emotionally ready to do so. Keep in mind that emotionally ready doesn't mean the absence of any kind of emotional distress. Emotionally ready means having awareness of the emotional forces at play in you and your partner's minds as well as an awareness of the effect of resuming sexual activities on these forces. Be aware of how you and your partner currently feel and what the impact of resuming sexual activities will be on those feelings and whether or not you and your partner are able to mitigate that impact successfully without interfering with the healing process. So, if you are going to engage in physical intimacy, make sure that you are ready for its emotional effects and that you are doing it for the right reason. Doing it for the right reason means doing it because you have the emotional and physical desire to do so versus out of obligation and fear.

I also encourage the betrayed to make a distinction between making changes for the right reasons versus making them because of comparisons. In other words, it's okay to make needed changes to satisfy your partner sexually. Doing so does not mean that you are copying the third party. It simply means that you are providing for the needs of your partner. The rule of thumb here is that those changes have to make sense to you in terms of their validity and whether or not they conflict with who you are.

Physical Barriers

The physical barriers toward restoring physical intimacy can be summarized in two categories: legitimate health concerns and worries about sexual performance. In regard to the legitimate health concerns, couples usually struggle with the fears of unwanted pregnancies and sharing sexually transmitted diseases. I always recommend that my couples reach an agreement for a thorough health assessment to rule out any of these physical concerns. It's important for the betrayed to feel physically safe and secure prior to resuming sexual activities. Keep in mind that there are many ways to conduct such health evaluations. Be sure to opt for the one that is most suited for your needs.

The worries about sexual performance can become a physical barrier when the unfaithful and the betrayed are distracted by the negative emotions caused by the affair. It's common for couples to report sexual performance issues as a result of preoccupation with the insecurity, intrusive thoughts and images, and the need for comparison. This is why I recommend to my couples that when they make the decision to resume sexual activities, they must manage their expectations, especially when considering that they are trying to overcome a variety of obstacles. This is the time to focus on the significance of being able to resume sexual activities rather than focusing on how great it is.

Healing Pain of Generalization of Doubt

In the majority of cases, the betrayed is usually caught off guard with the news of the affair. Feeling surprised by the news would be an understatement. It's usually feelings of shock and disbelief, especially in the cases in which there were no obvious signs for dissatisfaction in the relationship.

Needless to say, the experience shakes the reality of the betrayed and makes them question everything. This is based on the fact that they are no longer able to trust their own perception about the relationship. Because, up to the point of finding out about the affair, they were operating under the belief that all is well or all is not bad enough that they felt the need to worry about an affair.

The over generalization of doubt takes place when the betrayed becomes obsessed with reexamining the entire timeline of the relationship looking for clues or gaps that might be indicative of wrongdoings. This takes the form of questioning and interrogating the unfaithful about past events that are unrelated to the affair. The betrayed's preoccupation with this mentally and emotionally draining task persists, even when the unfaithful are honest and forthcoming with the story of the affair and its timeline.

The process of doubting and questioning can cause more conflict between the partners because the unfaithful will feel frustration and helplessness over the betrayed's obsession. This is especially true if the unfaithful were forthcoming about everything that took place. This makes them wonder if it would be easier to make up stuff that didn't happen just to appease the betrayed's persisting doubts.

The best way to overcome this healing pain is by making a conscious choice to move forward and measure the quality of the relationship and the dedication of each partner based on future behaviors. What I emphasize to the betrayed is that the awfulness of the affair does not negate the authenticity and goodness of the relationship prior to its occurrence. I also emphasize that if the doubts are caused by disbelief of the unfaithful's timeline and story, then you should revisit *Milestone Number Two: Getting the Story* to make sure it was done correctly.

Healing Pain of Holidays and Anniversaries

It's very common for couples to re-experience the trauma of the affair at a high intensity during periods of anniversaries and holidays. I use the analogy of the process of grief and how people re-experience the painful impact of the loss with every anniversary and holiday that passes without the presence of the deceased loved one.

In the case of infidelity, the couples are grieving the loss of the relationship they had prior to the affair. Holidays and anniversaries become a painful reminder of what they used to have and what was lost. So it's only logical to feel sad, angry, resentful, and so on.

The good news here, is that the intensity of the pain associated with grief lessens with the passage of time because, after all, we are very adaptable creatures. Furthermore, there is one major difference between losing a person to death versus losing a state of satisfaction in a relationship. The first one is irreversible, but the second one has a chance of resurrection and improvement.

My advice to couples who are struggling with this issue is to plan ahead for these anniversaries and holidays. You do it by preparing yourself mentally for what to expect and creating a plan on how to deal with those feelings as a couple. It's also important to internalize the belief that your relationship did not die. It was damaged. Despite the severity of this damage, you have the potential to rebuild it to be even better than it was before the affair. This means instead of mourning the loss of past memories, focus on creating newer, happier memories.

Healing Pain of Grieving the Loss of the affair

This particular healing pain is very challenging for both the unfaithful and the betrayed. This is based on the fact that it's an unavoidable, necessary, yet nasty pill to swallow. This is especially true in the emotional and mixed type of affairs, in which there is a strong emotional bond between the unfaithful and the third party. Severing such a bond, regardless of desire to do so, and the firm belief in needing to do it, is not going to be an easy process.

The struggle for the unfaithful manifests in the guilt about the unnecessary pain they have caused the third party, because they got them to be emotionally involved, and now they are going back to rebuild their marriage. Another struggle for the unfaithful is the fact that they will miss the pleasant aspects they enjoyed about the affair, but paradoxically feel bad for having those feelings. It's the same kind of feeling you get when you quit something that is bad for you, but was also an enjoyable thing to do. Except here, this thing is not a thing; it's a real human being with their own thoughts and emotions.

What I tell the unfaithful is to allow themselves to experience these feelings of loss openly instead of suppressing them. Because, pretending that you don't have those feelings is not going to make them go away, it will just ensure that they will intensify and come out in weird, unproductive ways. The key is to share those feelings in a sensitive way that takes in consideration the feelings of the betrayed, which can be accomplished by continuously expressing and showing dedication to the rebuilding process.

This means that you and your partner will have to agree on the expected and appropriate expression of such feelings. You also need to create a safe environment for expressing those feelings. It's also important to know how much involvement the betrayed wants to have in witnessing and helping with processing those feelings. This is based on the fact that most of the time, it's difficult for the betrayed to sympathize with the unfaithful when it comes to their struggle with the loss of the third party. It's unfair and unrealistic to expect the betrayed to be a crying shoulder for the unfaithful in regard to the loss. So what I ask the betrayed for in this situation is understanding rather than sympathy. I also encourage the use of individual counseling to help the unfaithful get the support they need to process their feelings of loss.

The struggle for the betrayed takes place when they witness the impact of that loss on the unfaithful. The betrayed usually misinterprets the mourning of that loss as an indicator of the lack of the unfaithful's dedication to rebuilding the relationship. Sometimes, mourning the loss gets misinterpreted as an indicator that the unfaithful is really in love with the third party and, therefore, should not be attempting to rebuild. Overall, witnessing the mourning of loss impacts the betrayed's security and optimism about the relationship rebuilding efforts.

What I explain to the betrayed is the importance of allowing the unfaithful to mourn the loss of the affair, because it will allow them to put it in the past. Failing to do so will lead to the interference of those unresolved feelings with the progress of rebuilding the relationship. Mourning the loss is the healthy thing to do as long as the couple is in agreement about the appropriate ways to mourn that loss, which should not include any attempts of contact once that door to the third party is closed.

It's also helpful for the betrayed to make a distinction between the emotional attachment developed between the unfaithful and the third party and the emotional attachment between the unfaithful and the betrayed. The emotional bond developed in the affair is not as strong as the one developed in a real relationship. This is based on the facts we discussed in previous chapters, which is affairs are not real relationships, but are relationship proxies. Meaning, any feelings that develop within the context of the affair should be seen and measured in that light. It's like the difference between infatuation and real love. The first one is easily obtained, quick, superficial, and born out of impulse and desperation making it less likely to survive hardships. The second one is earned, matured over time, and born out of conviction and trust, which makes it strong enough to survive adversity.

Now, keep in mind that in some instances of infidelity, the unfaithful does find true love in the affair instead of just infatuation. In those circumstances the unfaithful has to come up with a very good reason of why they are sacrificing that love to rebuild their relationship with the betrayed. Furthermore, the betrayed will have to be willing to accept the idea that just because the unfaithful was capable of loving someone else, it does not negate their ability to be in love with them.

Healing Pain of Double Standard of Emotional Experience

One of the challenges associated with the process of healing from infidelity is the fact that life goes on while you are in the midst of the healing process. This means that even though you and your partner are diligently working on the action plan, you are still going to be making each other mad in ways that have nothing to do with the affair and the process of healing from it. This is based on the fact that neither of you were perfect human beings before the affair, and working on an action plan is not going to change that.

The problem takes place when the betrayed develops the double standard of who is allowed to experience frustration and pain. Naturally, after an affair, the betrayed feels that they have a monopoly on pain, frustration, and suffering because they are the victim of the affair. Even though it's understandable why the betrayed feels this way, it's not a realistic expectation, because, despite the awful past actions of the unfaithful, the unfaithful still has normal feelings that can get hurt just like everyone else. If we say that they are not allowed the privilege to have such experiences, then we are setting them up for failure because nothing good comes out of bottling up your feelings.

The reason why the betrayed feels that they should have a monopoly often stems from the need to punish or the need to assure that the unfaithful earns forgiveness. As mentioned in previous chapters, I am all for the idea of assuring that people experience the natural consequences of their behavior as long as those consequences are appropriate to the act and conducive to healthy functioning. I have the same stance toward earning forgiveness and redemption and the necessary acts needed to achieve that goal. The only problem here is that taking someone's needed right to experience pain and suffering is not going to achieve those goals nor is it a healthy limit to set in the relationship.

My advice to couples is to allow themselves to experience the wide emotional rainbow as long as those feelings are appropriate to the situation, communicated clearly, and expressed in a healthy manner that is conducive to conflict resolution

Healing Pain of Over-Correction

When people try to make changes in general, they struggle with finding balance. They either go over or under the point where they actually need to be. One of the ways this tendency plays out is through the unfaithful's and sometimes the betrayed's exaggerated attempts to be a better partner. Both behaviors are motivated by fear. The unfaithful is afraid that he or she will lose the betrayed if they don't try hard enough. The betrayed is afraid that if he or she doesn't forgive quickly or change the issues that led to the affair, then the unfaithful will decide to quit the efforts to rebuild. The observable manifestation of both of these fears is usually described as "trying too hard" or "being too clingy."

The best way to overcome this particular healing pain is by prevention, which can be achieved by developing and sticking to a clear action plan that outlines specific, expected changes. But, if you fail in prevention, the next best thing is early identification of any sings of over-correction followed by a healthy discussion that would facilitate solutions to achieve balance. It's also important for couples to avoid misinterpreting over-correction with bribing or phony attempts to regain favor. This determination can only be achieved if you and your partner are honest with yourself and each other about the motivations behind your actions.

A successful implementation of the action plan is key to surviving the healing pains caused by the affair. Following the rules of implementation will help you achieve your goals and assure that you and your partner are staying on the path. The completion of this milestone will get you closer to your final destination, but it does not mean that your work is done. Once you succeed in achieving your goals, you must continue your efforts to sustain that success for the long run, which will be discussed in detail in the next and final chapter.

Chapter 10

The Seventh Milestone:
Monitoring and Sustainability

"Our love is like a tree that grows still stronger
through the years nourished by our laughter and
sometimes by our tears."

---Author Unknown

Finally, you have arrived at the last milestone of the healing process. You have come a long way to get to this point and invested a lot of time, energy, and effort to achieve all this progress, so it only make sense to have the last milestone centered on helping you maintain what you have achieved.

What is Sustainability?

Sustainability is traditionally defined as possessing the ability to keep things at a certain level, or, in other words, maintaining the status quo. When it comes to healing from infidelity in particular and overcoming relationship struggles in general, I require all my clients to extend that definition beyond the traditional scope. I believe that sustainability should not be a passive process solely focused on preventing the loss of the grounds you gained. It should be a proactive process that is aimed at protecting what you have achieved as well as striving to improve it. This is why I encouraged all my clients to incorporate two important adjectives to ameliorate their sustainability efforts, which are eternal, and dynamic.

Eternal Sustainability

One of the first things I do before taking on new clients is assess their willingness to not only make the changes necessary to achieve relationship satisfaction, but also the willingness to put forth the effort to maintain those changes once they are achieved. Having this requirement sets the stage for couples to be educated about the reality of what it takes to be in a happy relationship, which requires ongoing work and effort. There are many couples who are misinformed about what is needed to obtain and sustain relationship satisfaction. They usually fall into two categories: the "all you need is love" category and the "set it and forget" category.

The couples in the "all you need is love" category operate under the misconception that relationship satisfaction is something that you stumble upon or something that simply happens organically without any work or effort as long as you love one another. These couples are usually flying blind and not paying attention to their needs as individuals and as couples. The couples in the "set it and forget it" category are operating under the misconception that relationship satisfaction requires *some* work and effort, but once satisfaction is achieved its going to be self-sustaining without any further conscious attempt or efforts to maintain relationship satisfaction. These couples are often dumbfounded when they start drifting apart as the result of a decline in their relationship satisfaction because form their perspective they did the work needed to achieve happiness already and now are confused about why they lost it.

Healing from infidelity is aimed at achieving relationship satisfaction. This is why it's important for you and your partner to embrace the concept of eternal sustainability, especially when considering the enormous amount of effort it took to get to this point. I always give the analogy of plate spinning when discussing the concept of sustaining relationship satisfaction.

In a plate spinning act, the performer has to continuously monitor and spin each plate to make sure that it remains balanced on the poles. The moment the performer blinks or gets distracted, one or more plates will fall and break. So, if you want to be happy and satisfied in your relationship, your efforts will need to continue beyond reaching the goals of satisfaction and getting out of the doghouse. You can't stop monitoring and spinning just because you did enough work to get the plates balanced. The moment you stop assessing your relationship and making the proper adjustments to keep it healthy is the same moment in which you will begin to lose all the work you invested in repairing it.

Dynamic Sustainability

Relationships are similar to living organisms in the sense that they have a life of their own, and that life is heavily influenced by its surroundings. In order for living organisms to survive and thrive, they must have the proper healthy environment to grow as well as the ability to adapt to the constant changes in their environment.

Dynamic sustainability is embracing the idea of making your sustainability efforts adaptable to the constant changes in your relationship environment instead of just focusing those efforts on keeping the status quo. Because, if your sustainability efforts are static and not keeping up with new changes in your life, they will cease to be effective in maintaining your relationship satisfaction.

Think of it this way, when we are young and healthy, we have a high metabolism, which means maintaining a particular weight can be achieved by a moderate amount of exercise and healthy diet. But, as we get older, our metabolic rate decreases, and the type of exercise that once worked for maintaining our weight will no longer be as effective, even if you maintain the same healthy diet. This means that if you want to continue maintaining your weight at a certain level, you must change your exercise regimen to keep up with the change in your metabolism.

Dynamic sustainability is basically the same idea; you want to make sure that what it takes to maintain the relationship satisfaction is keeping up with the new changes in you and your partner's life. Keep in mind that dynamic does not mean that your efforts will always have to increase. Dynamic simply means making the appropriate adjustment to account for the impact of the new changes in your life to assure successful maintenance of relationship satisfaction goals.

Aspiring for improvement instead of focusing only on maintaining the status quo is one of the best ways to assure that you are keeping up with life's changes. This is based on the fact that putting a cap on how much work you are willing to invest to maintain your relationship satisfaction will lead to future struggles if and when the time comes to raise that cap. It's always better to be prepared.

Achieving Sustainability

By definition, sustainability cannot take place without achieving the goals of healing from infidelity and reaching relationship satisfaction. Sustainability manifests through the conscious acts and efforts aimed at maintaining the progress gained from achieving your relationship goals. So, before you can begin the sustainability efforts, you and your partner must answer two questions: "How do we know we have achieved our goals?" and, "What do we need to do to maintain the progress gained from achieving our goals?"

How Do We Know We Have Achieved Our Goals?

This is one of the most important questions you and your partner should ask in order to solidify your efforts in the healing journey. Despite the significance of this question, many couples struggle to find a concrete or agreed upon answer. This is usually due to the fact that the short-term goals of earning forgiveness and rebuilding trust, as well as the long-term goals of relationship satisfaction, are concepts that are difficult to quantify in a tangible, measurable way. This is why I put a lot of emphasis on creating the action plan, which, if done correctly, will provide you with the specific and concrete indicators of goal achievement. Those indicators will let you know whether or not you have achieved your goals.

In addition to the action plan discussed in previous chapters, you and your partner need to develop a baseline for your relationship satisfaction. A baseline is a reference point used to measure and calculate certain levels. In this case, the baseline will measure the level of relationship satisfaction. Having that reference point will allow you to identify whether or not you are at the level you desire and, if not, how far you are from that level. So, not only will it let you know whether or not you have achieved your goal, it will also work as a compass that will come in handy in case you veer away from your destination. In order to develop a useful baseline, the two of you have to clearly define what a happy and satisfied relationship looks like to each of you.

An important thing to consider when developing a baseline is that it should be suited to your needs during the timeframe that you intend to use it. In other words, the baseline for relationship satisfaction prior to the affair might not be an appropriate baseline to use after the affair. This means that you and your partner have to always modify this baseline to suite your relationship needs and the changes in your life. This will assure that the reference point you are using to gauge where you are is relevant and accurate.

One of the related questions to the question of, "How do we know we have achieved our goals?" is, "How long is it going to take us to get there?" This is a question that preoccupies the minds of all couples trying to heal from infidelity. The preoccupation with timeframe is usually motivated by the need to end the suffering and put the whole ugly business behind them.

Unfortunately, there is no magic answer that works for everyone, especially when considering that each relationship has its own set of unique variables. Furthermore, there are many different forces at play that can either prolong or shorten the healing period significantly. Some of these forces are related to the affair in terms of the type of affair, causes of the affair, duration of the affair, the impact of the affair, and the couple's past history. Other factors are related to the couple's commitment to the healing process in terms of dedication of time and choosing the right kind of professional help. In addition to that, one must also consider the individual process of each partner from their perspective as the unfaithful or the betrayed as well as their own individual strengths and weaknesses that are not related to the affair but might play a major role in speeding up or slowing down the healing process.

So when couples ask me how long it's going to take to completely heal, I usually say as long as it takes you to complete all of the milestones successfully. I've seen recovery periods as short as three months and as long as eighteen months. Bottom line, you get from it what you put into it. So, don't focus on the number of weeks and months. Instead, focus on how successful you are in completing each milestone.

What Do We Need to Do to Maintain the Progress Gained from Achieving Our Goals?

Planning ahead is one of the best strategies that you can use to increase your chances of maintaining relationship satisfaction reached at the end of your healing journey. Just as you developed an action plan to make the changes needed to heal and be happy in your relationship, you will need to develop and implement an action plan for sustaining that happiness and satisfaction. The sustainability plan should include two types of measures: prevention and intervention. Both measures will require you to utilize the following skills: early identification, effective communication, and solution development.

Prevention

Preventative measures are actions designed to prevent a relapse into old habits and patterns of behavior that are not conducive to healthy functioning and relationship satisfaction. It was Benjamin Franklin who said, "An ounce of prevention is worth a pound of cure." That statement is apt when it comes to the role of preventative measures in helping couples maintain a healthy and happy relationship. Identifying the preventative measures you and your partner should use to prevent relapses will save the two of you a lot of unnecessary pain and heartache. This is why I encourage all my clients who are at this milestone to take the time to create and practice these preventative measures on a regular basis to combat complacency. There are many tools couples can use to take preventative measures, but here is a list of the most important ones that you must have in your toolbox:

Early Warning Signs

One of the most common statements I hear from the betrayed is, "I never saw this coming," or "I didn't see any warning signs." These statements reflect the couple's failure to identify a clear baseline that can be used to measure the health of the relationship, meaning, if couples were crystal clear on what a normal, happy, and satisfied partner and relationship looked like, they would have been able to detect any signs of change in those areas.

Granted, some people are good at hiding or bottling up feelings of unhappiness and dissatisfaction, but that doesn't mean that there are no visible signs that can be used as an indicator of deviation from the level of satisfaction that you both seek and aspire to maintain. If you want to be successful in sustaining the progress you have achieved so far, then you and your partner will need to develop clear, early warning signs that can be used as an indicator that things are starting to veer off course.

The benefit of the early warning signs goes beyond its utility as a compass that can be used to make corrections. It also helps in building trust, because if the betrayed knows what early warning signs he or she needs to look for, they will feel a lot safer about the potential for relapse. This is based on the fact that detecting the early warning signs will allow an opportunity to make correction before the actual relapse.

There are a few important concepts that you need to consider while developing those early warning signs—one: the keyword here is early, meaning, you need a sign that can be used before the axe is dropped, not after the fact; two: early warning signs should be seen as a safety net rather than the first line of defense, meaning, early warning signs should not be a replacement for the first line of defense, which is the conscious act of expressing dissatisfaction directly rather than waiting for your partner to see a warning sign; and three: the early warning signs should be clear, agreed upon, and reflective of abnormal changes versus expected ones. In other words, there is a normal, accepted deviation from the agreed upon baseline that should not be a cause of concern. The early warning signs should be seen as changes that fall outside the normal, "we are not perfect every day" type of deviation.

Lastly, you and your partner need to agree to express and address those warning signs in a safe and respectful manner that will lead to resolution. This means that you need to make a commitment to assure that those early warning signs are going to be expressed well and received well. Make sure that it's not expressed in a punitive way, and make sure that it's not received with resentment and anger.

Perpetual awareness of self and others.

We are all guilty of letting life overwhelm us with all the responsibilities that come with the different roles we play. This is why we are operating on autopilot most of the time, even when we have a few moments away from those responsibilities. We often use those moments to "unplug." This constant preoccupation with life stressors often robs us from the opportunity to get in touch with our own feelings and thoughts which, subsequently, lead us to behave poorly. In addition to losing touch with our own feelings and thoughts, we also become blind and deaf to the thoughts and feelings of those around us, leading to poor attention and responses to their needs.

Think of it this way, one of the main contributing factors to relationship problems in general, and with infidelity in particular, is the lack of awareness of needs of self and partner. Getting in the habit of engaging in awareness of self and others will ensure that you are paying attention to the thoughts and feelings of yourself and your partner. That awareness will give you a goldmine of data that you can use to gauge where you are and where you need to be in terms of relationship satisfaction. This is why that awareness cannot be sporadic, because if you only check in on your progress once in a blue moon, you could risk drastic deviation from where you actually need to be. This is why awareness of self and others needs to be perpetual.

Furthermore, awareness of self and others is going to help you identify the new changes that you and your partner will undergo in life. We all grow and change and so do our needs and the way we want those needs fulfilled. Having that awareness will help you pinpoint these changes and help you adapt to them successfully.

Forward Thinking

Having a future oriented mindset is essential when it comes to the need for anticipating the effects of expected and unexpected variables in your life. Forward thinking doesn't just mean planning for worst case scenarios. It also means planning for future milestones and the accomplishments the two of you aspire to achieve as individuals and as a couple, because every change has an impact on your relationship satisfaction, even positive and planned changes like having a baby, buying a house, or getting a promotion.

The habit of planning ahead will ensure that you and your partner are calculating for the effects of the new variables that you may encounter in the future. Making that calculation will assure that you have a plan to make the necessary adjustments to avoid causing a decline in the relationship satisfaction that you have achieved. Another benefit of adopting a forward thinking attitude is the fact that it will strengthen the bond between you and your partner, because forward thinking will require creating plans to help each of you achieve the things that you desire as a couple and as individuals.

Working as a team to achieve individual and common goals increases solidarity.

Regular Check-Ins

The use of check-ins should be a part of the ongoing maintenance efforts of your relationship satisfaction. I encourage couples to have brief, specific check-ins daily, and comprehensive, detailed check-ins on a weekly or biweekly basis. In successful organizations where teamwork is part of the daily process, there is scheduled time on a regular basis for the team members to communicate with one another about everything that pertains to the success of the business.

The purpose of the check-in is to allow you and your partner to assess your level of satisfaction, address changes in needs, plan for future goals and challenges, give feedback, and create plans for corrections and adjustments. The benefit of check-ins should go beyond the sustainability of what you accomplished and extend to continuing your efforts to make things even better than they were.

Keep in mind that these check-ins don't have to be stuffy and boring like business meetings. You can make them fun and enjoyable for you and your partner. See it as an opportunity to work with your favorite person in the world to help each other sustain and continue to improve the mutual goal of relationship satisfaction. You can have your check-in on a nice walk or as a laid-back coffee or dinner date. Do it regularly to celebrate the successes and highlight areas that need improvement.

Intervention

Interventions are the actions that you and your partner should take whenever a relapse takes place. A relapse doesn't mean another affair. A relapse is making mistakes that the two of you have agreed to avoid making. It's the resurgence of old, unhealthy patterns of behavior or the remission of new, healthy patterns of behavior. A lot of couples make the mistake of assuming that any kind of relapse, no matter how big or small, will automatically translate to a complete loss of all progress gained. This is not a realistic nor productive outlook on the issue of relapse. Because, despite you and your partner's best efforts, you are bound to make some mistakes. What I encourage my clients to do is assess each mistake individually within the context of the overall progress and success before deeming the whole thing as a failure. In other words, don't throw the baby out with the bath water.

It's also important to remember that not every mistake lends itself to such analysis. After all, there are some redlines that should never be crossed at this point of time regardless of the circumstances. For example, a relapse in failing to show affection to your partner out of complacency or getting busy with life stressors can be managed and corrected even if this was one of the factors that contributed to the affair. Cheating on your partner again because of that failure to show affection, however, is a mistake that obliterates all the progress gained, and is an indication of a lack of dedication to the relationship, which translates to a negative outlook on the relationship's future chances for success.

Bottom line, interventions can help you sustain and salvage the progress you have achieved if the relapse was related to understandable, minor mistakes caused by a learning curve or momentary lapse in judgment or focus. But, the overall success of the intervention in helping you sustain the progress you have achieved depends on two factors: immediacy and aggressiveness.

Immediacy

Ideally you want to prevent relapses by paying attention to the early signs we discussed in the prevention section. Missing out on that opportunity drastically reduces the available time you have to make the necessary changes and adjustments to avoid further deterioration of the quality of the relationship after a relapse. This means that when relapses occur, they need to be addressed immediately. The longer you wait, the worse things will get, and the longer it will take to bounce back. When relapses take place, dealing with them should become the main priority in your life.

A lot of couples fail in creating and implementing interventions in a timely manner. The delay is usually caused by one or more reasons. One of the common reasons is complacency, which is fueled by thoughts like, "Things are not as bad as they seem," or "Things are not going to be perfect all the time." Another common cause of delay is letting life stressors get in the way of addressing the relationship problems. This is usually caused by failing to balance the responsibilities of the roles we play and failing to make the relationship satisfaction a main priority.

I always remind my clients that relationship problems start small but grow into bigger and more complicated problems. It's much easier to deal with and fix these problems when they are small, rather than waiting until they become unmanageable. I also emphasize that immediate intervention does not mean impulsive and irrational actions. It simply means making the need to deal with the relapse a main priority. In other words, time is important as long as we are able to be thoughtful and considerate about choosing the best course of action to take to deal with the relapse.

Aggressiveness

Another factor that will determine the success of your intervention is the potency of your actions. When I say aggressive, I mean use every resource available for you to deal with the relapse, instead of doing just the bare minimum. You and your partner have worked hard to achieve all this progress, which means that you have to protect it and fight for it with everything you have.

It's important to make the distinction that aggressive does not mean overkill. It simply means using the most effective tools to deal with the scale of the problem. For example, let's say you are trying to tear down a wall in your house and you have three tools that you can use to get the job done. Those tools are a chisel, a sledge hammer, and a wrecking ball, all of which will get the job done but only one is the most appropriate for this situation. Can you guess which one? Well, the answer is the sledge hammer, because the chisel will take forever and require a ridiculous amount of physical energy. The wrecking ball, on the other hand, is very fast, but too big for the job and risks damaging other parts of the house.

In summary, make sure that you and your partner make a thorough assessment of the scale of the relapse and choose the most effective measures to deal with it. Choose the measures that are guaranteed to achieve the maximum benefits instead of opting for the easier ones. I also encourage my clients to seek individual and couples counseling when they are dealing with relapses to assure that they are addressing it appropriately and minimizing the possibility of further decline in relationship satisfaction.

Final Words

My dear reader, this is the part where we say our goodbyes. But, before we do that, I want to thank you and your partner for embarking on this journey with me. I know that it wasn't easy for either of you, especially when considering all the difficulties you had to endure to get to this point. My only hope is that the knowledge shared with you during this journey, as well as the process of achieving the milestones, allowed you to mend your hearts and heal your relationship.

It has been my greatest pleasure and privilege to be your guide on this difficult journey. Healing from infidelity together or separately is one of the greatest achievements one can accomplish in life. Surviving this awful experience and learning from it will ensure that you can face whatever challenges life throws your way. This is why you have my utmost respect and admiration for all you have invested in this process so far.

Please feel free to reach out to me with any questions or feedback you may have about this book or your individual struggle with infidelity. You can contact me directly through the Infidelity Counseling Center (www.infidelitycounselingcenter.com) which I have created for the sole purpose of helping couples like you who are trying to heal from infidelity. There, you will find a wealth of resources and information that can further educate you about the healing process. You will also find a safe and confidential forum that was created for couples dealing with infidelity. In this forum, you can read about other couples' experiences, successes, and challenges. You can also share your own experience about what you learned and accomplished thus far.

Take care, be well, and never give up on finding your happily ever after.

Tracking Your Progress

The First Milestone: Setting the Stage for Healing
- Make a conscious choice to heal.
- Agree on the logistics.
- Anticipate and prepare for challenges.
- Seek professional help.

The Second Milestone: Getting the Story
- Create a safe environment for proactive transparency.
- Suspend your disbelief.
- Control the content of the story.
- Move forward when the true story is told and revealed.

The Third Milestone: Acknowledging the Impact
- Assess the damage of infidelity.
- Articulate your understanding of the impact of infidelity.
- Validate the emotional experiences caused by infidelity.
- Take responsibility for the damages you have caused.
- Provide a sincere apology.
- Ask how you can support your partner in dealing with the impact.

The Fourth Milestone: Choosing a Path
- Identify the obstacles preventing you from choosing a path.
- Assess your relationship history prior to the affair.
- Identify the type and actual causes of your affair.
- Assess your performance in the previous milestones.
- Use your findings to choose a path.

The Fifth Milestone: Creating a Plan of Action
- Reach consensus of choice.
- Clarify the true motives behind your choice.
- Express your intention, and provide disclosure.
- Choose a start time for implementation.
- Develop clear, short-term and long-term goals.
- Develop concrete steps and measurable indicators.

The Sixth Milestone: Implementation and Healing Pains
- Stick to the plan.
- Show your work.
- Avoid misperceptions.
- Assess your progress, revaluate, and make adjustments.
- Be patient and empathetic.
- Understand and prepare for healing pains.

The Seventh Milestone: Sustainability
- Develop early warning signs.
- Engage in perpetual awareness of self and others.
- Adopt a forward thinking attitude.
- Schedule regular check-ins.
- Understand and plan for relapses.
- Develop immediate and aggressive interventions.

Made in the USA
Coppell, TX
12 March 2020